BLACK DOG COTTAGE COOKBOOK
Adie McClelland

PHANTOM
HOUSE

BLACK DOG COTTAGE COOKBOOK
Adie McClelland

PHANTOM HOUSE

Acknowledgements

Many thanks to the following people for their assistance and support. In alphabetical order:

Clint Black, Chris Brown, Caroline Cheetham, Richard and Sarah Caughley, David Gascoigne, Ann Clifford, Cheryll Goodley, Clare Gordon, Sarah Hall, David Hendry, Ian Hornblow, Janie Miller, Helen Milner, Gabrielle McKone, Julie Muir, Sarah Philp, Patsy Reddy, Nicola Saker, Annabel Sinclair-Thomson, Darryn Smith, Paula Tata, Craig Walden, Mark & Vicky Williams, and Cameron Williamson.

Special thanks to Anna Symmans with whose encouragement, support and help made this book possible for me.

Principal photography by Grant Sheehan © www.grantsheehan.com

Additional photography by Matthew McClelland, Adie McClelland, Maisy McClelland, and Kieran Scott.

Text by Adie McClelland. www.adiemcclelland.co.nz

Edited by Shelley-Maree Cassidy.

Designed by Typeface Ltd. www.typeface.co.nz

Printed in China by Toppan Printing Co., (China) Ltd.

First published in 2009 by Phantom House Books Ltd ©
PO Box 6385 Marion Square, Wellington, New Zealand

E mail info@phantomhouse.com www.phantomhouse.com

Copyright © 2009 by Phantom House Books.

All rights reserved; no part of the contents of this book may be reproduced in any form without the permission of the publisher.

ISBN 978-0-9582838-5-4

Lovingly dedicated to my Mother, Joan and to my Mother-in-law, Philly.

Contents

Introduction 7

Mezze 11

Soups 35

Light Dishes 47

Family & Friends 81

Ode to Doris 110

Sweet Things 121

Essentials 143

Index 158

Maisy's Greek dancer.   Taken from her 2002 diary.

Larkin Street
Wadestown
Wellington

Dear Adie,

I always knew that one day my boat would come in!

I expect that for the rest of my life I will regard enrolling my bride in your cooking courses as one of the best investments I have ever made.

Not only is she now an accomplished cook but she has a passion for good food and cooking which she previously regarded as mundane.

Of course nothing is perfect. This weekend I had to convert an old broom handle into a rail above the stove. This is so she can hang her utensils on meat hooks so our kitchen looks just like yours.

Lots of love
Richard

Introduction

My cooking career began under false pretences many years ago in the port of Piraeus, Greece. As a young girl I bluffed my way into a job cooking on a charter yacht. It was a big step up for me from cooking for the shearers on the family farm in Orari in the South Island of New Zealand, but I got away with it and the experience has influenced my life and cooking ever since.

That summer my days revolved around the fresh produce we bought every day in the markets of the delightful Greek villages we visited. I started to cook local dishes, copying food we were eating in the seaside tavernas. The food was real peasant fare, nothing fancy but stunning. The tastes were so clean and it was all so simple. The same big bold earthy flavours kept coming though: the dense taste of tomatoes ripened in the intense heat, the pungent aroma of oregano picked from the hillsides and the heady flavour of a good glug of locally produced olive oil underlying every dish. I was hooked.

Later, my years spent in Hong Kong introduced me to another cuisine that delighted my senses and suited my cooking style. Asian food is wonderfully different but there's no longer any mystery to its prep thanks to well-stocked Asian sections in most supermarkets. The sour-hot and salty-sweet flavours of Asia are fabulously addictive and work so well for the passionate home cook.

So this book represents my travels and my favourites. This is the food I love to cook, the food I love to eat, the food I love to teach. It's food designed for relaxed and happy times with family and friends, eaten without ceremony and always enhanced with a good bottle of wine!

And this is what the Black Dog Cottage Cookbook is all about.

The name and overall flavour of this book come from my two favourite places in the world: Hydra, an island in the Greek Saronic Gulf and our bach at Mangakuri Beach in Hawke's Bay. Our beach hideaway is called "Mavros Skilos Cottage" which translated from the Greek means "Black Dog Cottage". These are where we have some of our best times and food is all part of it, every time.

Everyone can cook. But the more we cook and the more we experiment, the more we learn how flavours and textures work together and how food will respond to different ways of cooking. The more we learn the more confident we become at trusting our own instincts. So please don't slavishly follow these recipes, instead take them as guidelines. Be as loose and free with them as you wish, adapt them as you see fit and in this way you will make the food your own.

Cooking invariably ends up taking up a bit of time so I tend to lean towards recipes that don't take all day to prepare. I like my food to be fresh, clean, not over-handled and to have different layers of taste which unfold as you eat. Many of my recipes benefit from being made the day before, allowing the flavours to mellow and blend together. But there are plenty of recipes in this book designed to be prepared and cooked quickly so that all the flavours and textures remain fresh and light. Mediterranean and Asian food is where I always seem to end up.

I believe it's important to cook with produce which is in season and the return to farmers' markets and the revival of the vege garden are making this more and more a happy reality. Imported out-of-season produce is often disappointing and expensive. I love the rapport you can build with the vege man, the fishmonger and butcher. They are specialists and know exactly the origins and the finer points of the food they are selling you. The more time you spend with them, the more they will look out for you and you will build the sort of connection which seldom happens in a supermarket.

So, welcome to my favourite recipes. They are all tried and true. They are all simple – if they weren't, they didn't make the cut. They will feed anyone or everyone. Dress them up or dress them down. I hope you enjoy them.

I love cooking. It centres me, calms me and delights me. I love sharing my cooking with friends and family. I love the togetherness of sitting round the table with a steaming dish in the middle and knives and forks at the ready.

Happy cooking to you.

Adie McClelland

ΠΑΝ ΕΛΕΝΑ ΛΥ 981

Mezze

In most European countries it is not done to drink alcohol without food. Serving small snacks, hot or cold with drinks, can be mouthful treats that can easily become your desired way of eating for the entire meal. A single mezze can easily stand in for an entrée. Think of them as building blocks to your meal ahead. For this reason I normally only serve one mezze keeping it uncomplicated, simple, and using the best and freshest ingredients.

BLACK DOG COTTAGE COOKBOOK

My Greek Octopus

It would be difficult for me to eat octopus and not think of Greece. Octopus at Mangakuri are usually hauled up in the crayfish pots and having eaten the entire contents of the pot I have found that the taste of our octopus has a faint crayfish flavour.

Serves 4 (using a 1.5kg octopus)

Method

1. Before cooking the octopus you need to take the contents of the head out. To do this simply turn the head inside out and empty what's inside, then return it back to its normal shape. Of course this is always done for you if you are lucky enough to buy an octopus from your local fishmonger. The Greeks eat the head and I must say I like it too, so do give it a try.
2. Fill a large saucepan with water and add a drop of vinegar. Place the octopus in the water and bring to the boil. Simmer gently for about 45 minutes. Test for tenderness by poking a fork through the thickest part of the tentacles. It may require a little longer. Lift it out, when it is cool enough rub your fingers along the tentacles to remove the skin and suckers.
3. Chop into bite-sized pieces, discard the eyes and cut the head up as well.
4. Make up a little dressing of the juice of half a lemon, 2 tablespoons of your best extra virgin olive oil, and salt and pepper. Pour this over the octopus and leave it to marinate for a couple of hours. You can sprinkle over a little herb if you wish, but our octopus has a softer taste than the Greek octopus and a herb can often take over the subtle flavour.

Greek octopus

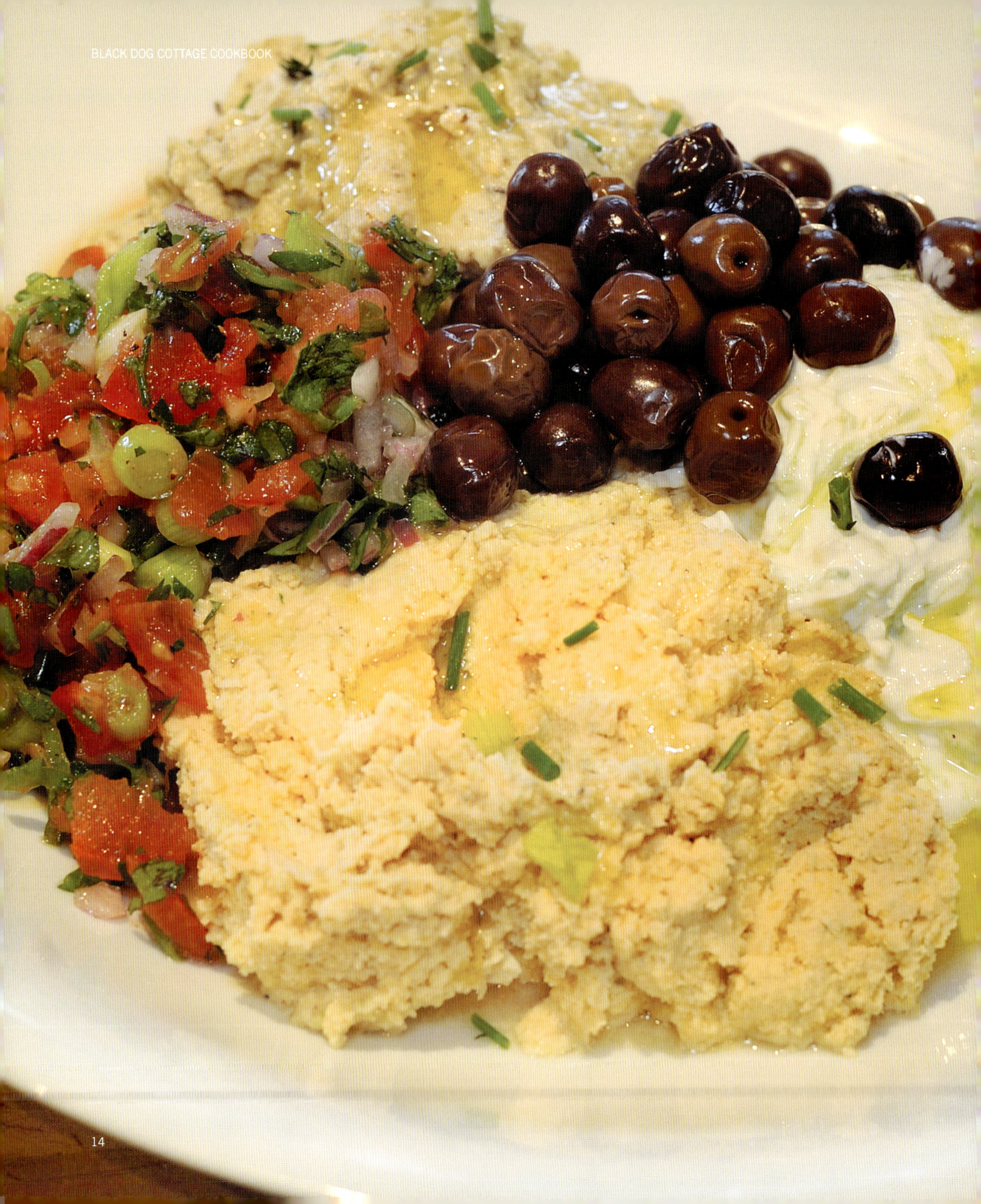

Mezze Plate of Baba Ghanoush, Hummus, Tzatziki, Roasted Olives and Tomato Salad

This mezze plate is stunning and certainly worth the effort. What makes it special is having all these combinations and flavours together. They serve it like this at the Bathers' Pavilion in Sydney and it has always struck a note with me.

Serves 8

Baba Ghanoush:
6 medium eggplants
3 garlic cloves, crushed
2 tbsp tahini
½ tbsp cumin, roasted and ground
1 tbsp lemon juice
Sea salt

Method
1. Roast eggplants at 200°C for about 30 minutes. The skins should look blackened and flesh should be soft.
2. When cool, peel off skin and leave flesh to drain in a colander for 30 minutes.
3. Place garlic and eggplant in a food processor and mix to a smooth paste.
4. Add tahini, cumin, lemon juice and salt and blend.
5. Add a few spoonfuls of yoghurt to the finished dip for a lighter, creamier finish.

Tzatziki:
4 telegraph cucumbers
1 tsp sea salt
500g Greek yoghurt
2 garlic cloves, crushed
1 tbsp lemon juice
Ground white pepper

Method
1. Grate unpeeled cucumbers and place in a colander. Sprinkle with salt, leave to rest for 10 minutes. Squeeze the excess moisture out of the cucumber and place in a bowl.
2. Mix in the yoghurt, garlic and lemon juice, then season with pepper.

Hummus:

340g chickpeas, soaked overnight
4 garlic cloves
4 tbsp lemon juice
4 tbsp tahini
Sea salt

Method

1. Cover chickpeas with water and cook for about 1 hour, or until very soft. Drain, reserving cooking liquid.
2. Place chickpeas and garlic in a processor, then add about a third of a cup of cooking liquid and process until smooth.
3. Add lemon juice and tahini and mix well. You may need to add a little more cooking liquid. It thickens as it cools.
4. Season with more of anything if you think it needs it.

Tomato Salad:

10 ripe tomatoes, seeded and diced
8 spring onions
½ cup parsley, chopped
2 small red onions, diced
3 tbsp lemon juice
4 tbsp olive oil
Salt and pepper

Method

1. Combine all ingredients in a bowl.
2. Pile mezze on platter with roasted olives and serve with bread.

More often than not, the best food is the simplest.

For some of us, this is very hard. It is tempting to add just that little bit more. Often it is a good idea to walk away and come back later to taste the results again. In this time, the flavours have settled and are now starting to combine. Perhaps you may need to adjust the seasonings or add something more. But remember: the less you do with food, the better. Try to let the dish speak for itself.

Souvlaki

Souvlaki is the Greek word for small pieces of meat threaded on a skewer then grilled over charcoal. Always make more of these than you think you need; they get hoovered up pretty smartly. They are ideal party food and go beautifully with the mezze plate of baba ghanoush, hummus, tzatziki, and tomato salad (*see page 15-16*) between two pieces of bread. We take our little Hibachi barbecue to the river and grill these there – perfect outdoor food. In Greece they are made with pork, which is also very yummy. You do need a little fat in the meat, so that the cubes "knit" together when they are cooking. It is for this reason that I use the shoulder of lamb with its marbled fat and for me, it has a sweeter taste than the leg.

Serves 4-6

1.36 kg shoulder of lamb (de-boned)
1-2 lemons, juiced
3 large cloves of garlic, crushed
Salt and freshly ground pepper
100mls extra virgin olive oil
2 tsp dried oregano or thyme
Wooden skewers

Method

1. Dry meat on kitchen towel, then cube into smallish squares.
2. Whisk together lemon juice, garlic, salt, pepper, oil and herb. Taste here, you may need a little more oil, but you want the marinade to be more on the "lemony" side.
3. Pour over the lamb, mix with your hands, cover and refrigerate for at least 3-4 hours. While this is happening, soak wooden skewers in water to prevent burning.
4. Prepare your coals and wait until the coals are all white and glowing softly. You do not need high heat. Thread pieces of meat on to skewers, give them a squeeze with kitchen towel before placing over the coals. Grill for about 15 minutes, turning once.
5. Squeeze lemon and sprinkle some salt over the souvlaki before you hand them to your guests.

Zucchini Fritters – Greek Style

Little plates of these delicious fritters come out with your evening drink in Greece, along with Tzatziki (see page 15) and half a lemon to squeeze over. Slices of aubergine can be treated in the same way. This batter is great for coating anything from a prawn to larger pieces of fish.

Makes enough for 4-6
Batter
125g flour
½ tsp salt
¼ cup light olive oil
175ml warm water
1 ½ egg whites, beaten to soft peak
Light olive oil for frying
3 ½ zucchini, sliced

Method

1. Sift flour and salt into a deep bowl, whisk in oil and water. Leave batter to stand for at least 30 minutes. Whip egg whites until they are at soft peak stage, then fold gently into batter.
2. Heat oil in pan. Dip sliced zucchini into batter and then into oil. Do not crowd the pan as this will bring the temperature of the oil down. Shallow fry until the batter is a light brown and crisp. Sprinkle with salt and a quick squeeze of lemon.

I use fresh herbs to season my food a lot and I adore putting together bouquet garnis, which add beautiful herby flavours to the finished dish. I add salt and pepper last to enhance the flavours.

19

BLACK DOG COTTAGE COOKBOOK

Yára, Greece   July 19th, 2002

Dearest Maisy, (Scraps)

    Although I am so sad to have to
goodbye to you now, I know
ing to be friends for the r
and I will never for
l adventures we

snap!   ah!

20

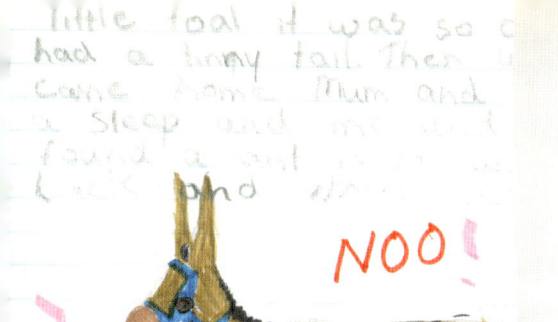

The surrounding cafes exhibit large shady awnings, but the ponies, mules and donkeys are forced to stand in the broiling sun

Donkeys dehydrate while authorities dither

Hydra's equine transport is applauded as eco-friendly and traditional, but the animals are left to wait long summer's days in full sun with no water due to bureaucratic indecision

By Cordelia Madden

THE TEMPERATURE is 39 degrees Celsius and rising. Not a cloud mars the peerless sapphire of the sky and the mid-summer sun burns fiercely. The visitors to Hydra's famously picturesque harbour laze under vast canopies sipping iced coffees and cool, glistening beer. Also keeping carefully in the shade are the owners of the donkeys, mules and ponies which provide the island's sole form of transport. Their animals, however, are not so fortunate. From 8am until 8pm they are constantly in full sun, alternately waiting on the harbourfront and toiling up and down Hydra's cobbled alleys.

While the businesses that operate around the Saronic island's port seem to have little trouble in gaining permission to erect much-needed shades, the area where the donkeys and ponies wait for custom remains completely unsheltered.

Although the mayor of Hydra has given his blessing to the construction of an awning for the working animals, it has not materialised. "Unfortunately we [the municipality] are not in a position to authorise the building of a shelter for the equines," says Constantinos Anastopoulos, Hydra's mayor.

Quibbling over shelter

The authority lies with the Ephorate of Classical and Byzantine Antiquities, a division of the culture ministry. "The whole of Hydra is listed as an archaeological site, so whatever is built needs to be agreed to by our service before it goes to the town planning commission," Charalambos Pennas, ephor with responsibility for the Cyclades and the Argo Saronic Gulf, tells the *Athens News*.

"The question of shade for the donkeys is a priority for any visitor, especially foreigners. But, though the mayor would like to appease these sensitive tourists by putting up a shelter, it's not such a simple proposition," he continues.

"It would be impossible to build a shelter large enough to accommodate all the animals," Pennas says, estimating that up to 70 equines work every day (the mayor puts the number as high as 300), "and therefore there would be the question of which donkeys and ponies went under the shade and which didn't."

Ignoring the suggestion that it could be on a first-come, first-serve or rotation basis, Pennas continues, "Also, in the summer months the harbourfront becomes very crowded and a corridor needs to be left open between all the shop-awnings and free-standing shelters for people to pass through. There simply wouldn't be room for a shady spot for the donkeys as well."

The ephor also says that the donkey owners are against the shelter, quoting them as dismissing the "ridiculous" idea and stating that it would be worse for the animals to wait in the shade and then have to go out directly into 45 degrees Celsius heat to work.

On the contrary, says donkey owner Anastasios Kokkos: "We all want the s... it will provide the animals with much-... protection."

Equine expert Janet Eley BVSc M... comments that even if they couldn't have... all day, it is crucial for the animals to ha... opportunity to wait out of the sun.

"They don't stand in the sun th... choice," she says. "Ponies can become... dehydrated, and although donkeys and... can tolerate longer periods in direc... without showing clinical signs of dehyd... they would always rather be in the shad...

When asked if he would consider ad... the ephor's idea of all the donkeys waiti... shady side-street until the boats ca... Kokkos is emphatically negative, addin... it would lose them valuable custom.

... ne'er a drop to drink

What the donkey owners consider t... problem of equal proportion to the l... shelter is the water situation. Although... Anastopoulos says that there is a fresh... supply on the harbour for the don... fishermen and yachts, Kokkos tells the ... News that the port authorities and munic... workers do not allow them to use the fa...

Deputy harbour master Yiannis B... disagrees, saying that as far as he is awar... is no objection to the donkey owners... water from this tap. "None of the owner... complained to us that they have been r... water," he adds.

"If they asked for water, they would ... says a municipal worker from the harbou... wishes to remain anonymous. "But the ... never even ask because they don't want t... to clean up donkey urine and faeces."

Whatever the reason the donke... ponies are not given access to water, ... fluids can seriously harm, and even kil... "Standing in the sun, equines get extr... dehydrated and need to be offered ... frequently," says Eley. "Feral donkeys... go to a water hole a couple of times a d... they would only be browsing and grazi... working a 12-hour shift. Equines that w... day need to be considered like athletes t... to get the conditions right - if they are ... and sweating in the sun, they are losi... water and minerals, and therefore n... replenish with electrolytes."

"The animals must be provided wit... and offered water regularly," she conc... "Otherwise they, especially the ponies... in danger of dehydrating to the point of

While their ponies suffer in the scorching heat, the owners enjoy a cigarette and a chat in the cool shade

Marinated Japanese Beef with Spring Onions

Excellent drinking nibbles – very moreish, so make plenty.

Makes about 16

375g fillet of beef
3 tbsp soy sauce
3 tbsp mirin or dry sherry
3 tbsp sugar
1 tsp finely grated fresh ginger
16 spring onions

Method

1. Cut the beef into very thin slices (3mm thick).
2. Mix soy sauce, mirin, sugar, and ginger until sugar dissolves. Pour onto a flat dish and marinate the beef slices for 20 minutes.
3. Cut the spring onions into pieces of a size that will leave some green portion and some white extending from each end when wrapped in beef. Wrap the beef around them and secure with a toothpick.
4. Grill the rolls over a pre-heated oiled grill or cook in a very hot frying pan lightly filmed with oil, turning them with tongs until brown.

When food has been in a marinade always lay it out on a kitchen towel and pat dry before you sear it or char-grill it. This prevents the food from "sweating" rather than searing and sealing.

Filo-Wrapped Asparagus And Parma Ham

This recipe came from Alastair Little. I have made this successfully with green beans when in season. A yummy nibble – easy, makes plenty and delicious to eat.

Serves 10
Filo pastry
Butter, melted
Grated Parmesan cheese
Thin slices of Parma ham
Asparagus

Method
1. Working with one filo sheet at a time, brush with some melted butter and fold over.
2. Sprinkle with parmesan.
3. Lay a slice or two of Parma ham on top, place an asparagus spear across and roll up.
4. Brush roll with butter.
5. Cut into lengths and bake at 230°C for 10 minutes until golden.

When melting butter in the microwave, tear off a piece of the butter wrapping and place in the bowl with the butter. This prevents the butter from spitting all over the inside of your microwave.

BLACK DOG COTTAGE COOKBOOK

Chickpeas with Tomato and Chilli

This recipe can be made two days ahead and stored covered in the refrigerator. Serve at room temperature with lots of crusty bread.

Serves 10

420g chickpeas, soaked overnight
3 bay leaves
3 sprigs of oregano
Olive oil
1 Spanish onion, finely chopped
3 cloves of garlic, finely chopped
3 fresh small red chillies, seeded and chopped
3 tomatoes, chopped and skinned
5 tbsp lemon juice, or to taste
1 tbsp oregano leaves
2 tbsp extra virgin olive oil

Method

1. Add drained chickpeas, bay leaves and oregano to a saucepan, cover with water and simmer for about 50 minutes or until soft. Drain and discard bay leaves and oregano.
2. Heat 2 tbsp olive oil in a large frying pan and cook onion over low heat until soft. Add garlic, chilli and tomato and cook, stirring occasionally, until the soft and pulpy liquid has evaporated. Remove from heat and stir in chickpeas.
3. Divide mixture in half. Process one half of mixture with 2 tbsp of lemon juice and a third of a cup of olive oil until smooth. Season to taste.
4. Add remaining lemon juice, 2 tbsp olive oil and 2 tsp of the oregano leaves to remaining chickpeas, season to taste and mix well.
5. To serve, spread puréed chickpea mixture over serving plate and top with whole chickpea mixture. Sprinkle with remaining oregano leaves and drizzle with extra virgin olive oil.

Asian Prawn Fritters

These little fritters go beautifully with a glass of bubbles or a crisp cold Pinot Gris. Serve with Lime and Chilli Syrup (see *Essentials*) or some sweet chilli sauce.

Makes 16-20

Batter:
⅓ cup water

½ cup fish stock

2 tsp salt

1 cup rice flour

¼ cup cornflour

Freshly ground pepper

2 eggs, beaten

1 tbsp finely grated ginger

1 medium sized onion, peeled and grated

1 cup bean sprouts

1 small sweet potato, peeled and grated

4 spring onions, sliced finely

1 tbsp chopped coriander

250g raw school prawns, shells and heads removed, tails left on

For frying the fritters:
Peanut oil – enough to shallow-fry

Method
1. Beat all ingredients for the batter together until smooth and add the vegetables and prawns.
2. Heat the oil in a pan until hot. Lift out spoonfuls of batter, making sure you have a prawn in the mix, and shallow-fry the fritters on both sides. Cook for about 2 minutes or until golden brown. Drain and serve.

To me, if a restaurant or a café has an interesting and well-put together antipasto or mezze plate, then they are well on their way to ensuring I am going to eat well. This is usually a true indication of what is going on in the kitchen.

Thai-High Chicken Livers

You will love this pâté with an Asian twist. It's exciting, different and very yummy.

Serves 8-12

1 tbsp peanut oil
1 tbsp butter
500g chicken livers
3 tbsp chopped shallots
¼ cup chopped spring onions
2 tsp finely chopped ginger
Salt and white pepper to taste
2 tbsp rice wine
2 tsp ground cumin
2 tbsp heavy cream
2 tbsp finely chopped water chestnuts
Fresh coriander, chopped

Method

1. Heat oil and butter. Add livers, sauté for 1 minute.
2. Add shallots, spring onions, ginger, salt and pepper and sauté for 1 minute.
3. Add rice wine, cumin and heavy cream. Sauté for a further 4-5 minutes, leaving livers slightly pink.
4. Stir in water chestnuts and remove from heat.
5. Cool to room temperature, then process.
6. Mix in chopped coriander.

BLACK DOG COTTAGE COOKBOOK

Thai Whitebait Fritters

I know you are thinking why would anyone do this to our beautiful whitebait but believe me, it's worth it, if only once. If you have some whitebait that has been in the deep freeze for too long, this would be a good way to use it up. I served this once with some steamed asparagus and sweet and sour cucumber relish (see *Essentials*) for lunch; fair to say it was an instant hit and those that were there are still talking about it! You could use the Asian whitebait for this recipe. It is cheaper and works well but it's wetter, so dry it as best you can on kitchen paper or a tea towel before putting it into the batter.

Serves 4

500g whitebait
3 tbsp chopped coriander
4 tbsp finely sliced shallots
1 tbsp fish sauce
Grated ginger to taste
1 tbsp finely chopped red chilli (no seeds) or 1 tbsp sambal oelek
Pinch of salt
200-250 ml vegetable oil

Batter:

1 cup self-raising flour
1 tbsp oil
1 tbsp vinegar
1 cup milk

Method

1. Combine whitebait, coriander, shallots, fish sauce, ginger, chillies, and salt.
2. Make batter by beating flour, oil, vinegar and milk together until smooth. Stand for 1 hour.
3. Heat vegetable oil in a deep pan until very hot. The amount of oil depends on your frying pan, but you want to make it deep enough so that the fritter isn't going to stick to the bottom.
4. Combine fish mixture with batter and drop spoonfuls into oil. The fritter will puff up slightly; turn over in the oil after a couple of minutes and fry on the other side. Lift out and drain well on a kitchen paper towel. Cut into this first fritter and check to see if the cooking time needs to be a little more or less. Remember never to crowd the pan as this will bring the heat of the oil temperature down and you will find that your fritter actually takes in oil rather than it "sealing" the outside.
5. Serve as soon as possible.

Pissaladiere

Great party nibble. Because of its firmer and crustier base this 'pizza' is ideal for drinks. Have fun and create your own combination for the topping.

Serves 4-6

Filling:

6 tbsp olive oil
6 cups sliced onions
2 tsp sugar
½ tsp salt
2 large garlic cloves, chopped finely
1 cup parsley and 2 anchovies blended together
Olives to garnish

Crust:

2 tsp yeast
½ cup water (warm)
1 tbsp olive oil
¾ tsp salt
½ tsp sugar
2 cups flour

Method

1. Heat olive oil, add onions, sugar and salt. Cook until golden brown. Add garlic. Cook until the mixture is slightly caramelised.
2. Combine yeast and quarter of the water. Stand 5 minutes. Add 1 tbsp olive oil, sugar and salt.
3. Add remaining water and flour and mix until smooth. Knead well for 3-4 minutes. Leave to rise for 1 hour.
4. Pinch and knead for 2 minutes. Leave to rise again.
5. Pre-heat oven to 180°C, roll dough then press into baking trays, spread parsley and anchovy paste over bottom. Pour onions over, dot with olives, drizzle oil over. Bake 45 minutes.

Look after your pans and knives. Avoid stacking pans on top of one another. Hang them if possible (what you want to avoid is scraping the surface of your pan). Knives should not be thrown into a drawer or poked down into one of those wooden blocks. This will blunt them. A knife rack is the best and most suitable way of caring for your knives.

31   Hydra

Seared Tuna in Soy and Mirin

For a quick easy snack, eat this raw or seared. It can also be made with salmon. Build it up to make a warm salad if you wish and serve with miso dressing (see *Essentials*), as it is here in the photograph.

Serves 4

450g fresh tuna
85ml Kikkoman soy sauce
85ml sunflower oil
85ml mirin
2 shallots, finely chopped
1 small chilli, seeds removed, chopped
1 dsp freshly chopped coriander
A little oil for searing

Method

1. Trim tuna to remove blood lines and cut into cubes. Place tuna in a bowl, add soy sauce, oil, mirin, shallots, chilli and the coriander. Toss tuna around in liquid to coat. Leave to marinate for 12-24 hours.
2. When ready to serve, remove tuna from marinade and dry. Retain marinade.
3. Heat a little oil to very hot and quickly sear the tuna on both sides, so that it remains very pink. Remove to a plate, drizzle some of the reserved marinade over, a grinding of pepper, and serve.

All meat and fish should be at room temperature before it is cooked.

Fava

This is a typical mezze all over Greece. Fresh bread and fava, very simple and extremely addictive.

Serves 4-6

370g yellow dal, rinsed thoroughly
1 small onion, left whole
3 cloves of garlic, left whole
2 bay leaves
Juice of ½ a lemon
1 large bunch of spring onions
1 tsp of fresh thyme
Salt and freshly ground black pepper
Your very best olive oil
Crusty bread to serve

Method

1. Place dal in a large saucepan with the onion, garlic and bay leaves. Cover with plenty of water and bring to the boil. Reduce to a simmer and stir occasionally. Cook for about 35 minutes or until the dal has become very soft. Skim off any scum.
2. Drain dal, keeping the cooking water. Remove bay leaves and onion and put the dal into a processor with peeled cooked garlic, 50ml of the cooking liquid and fresh lemon juice, and process until you have a very light, smooth pale mixture. Add more cooking liquid or some oil if it seems too stodgy. Taste and season with salt and pepper.
3. Chop the spring onions finely, including the green parts, and add to the fava along with the thyme.
4. Serve the fava on a large platter. Drizzle with a good glug of your very best oil and serve with the crusty bread.

"No mean woman can cook well, for it calls for a light head, a generous spirit and a large heart"
Paul Gauguin

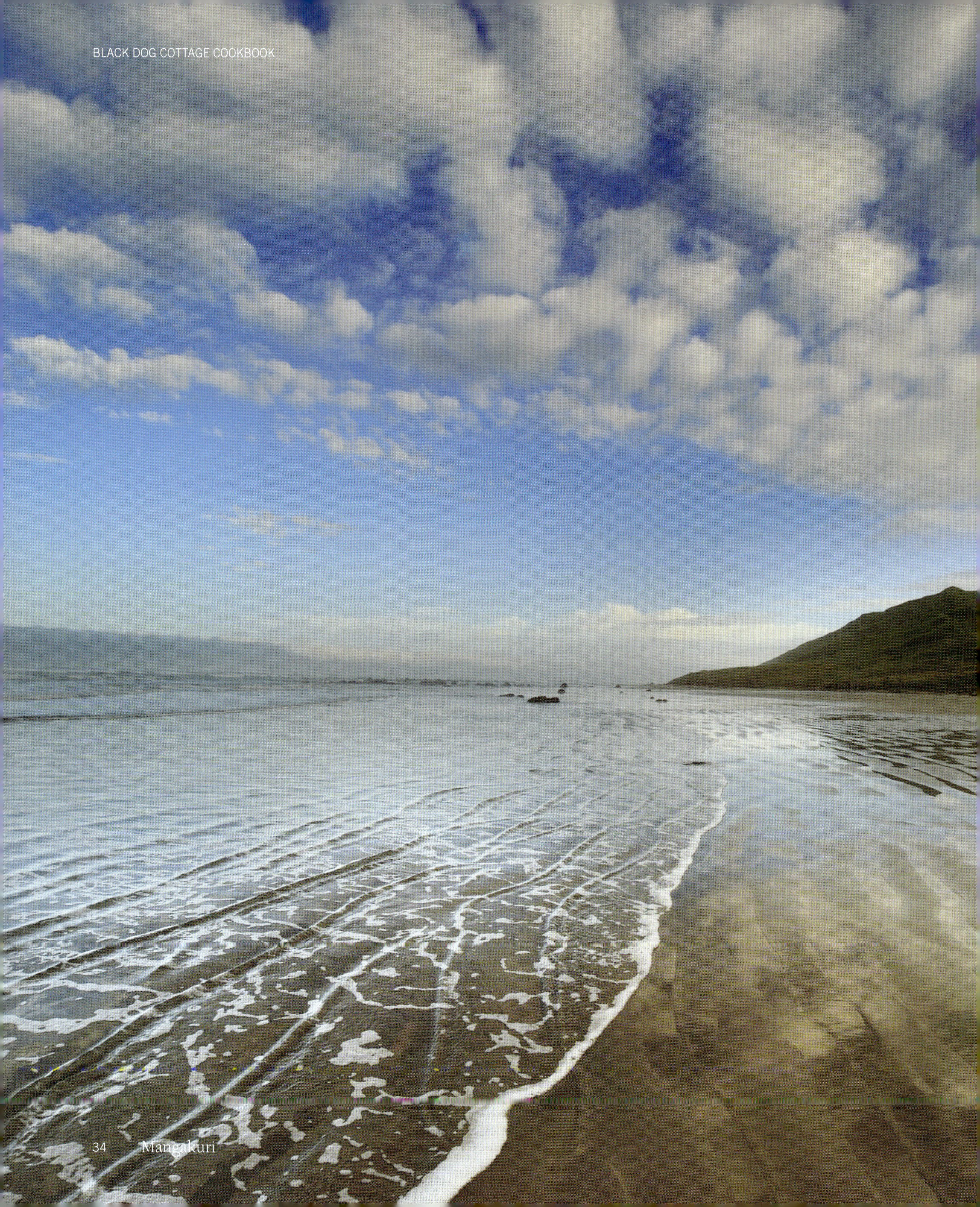

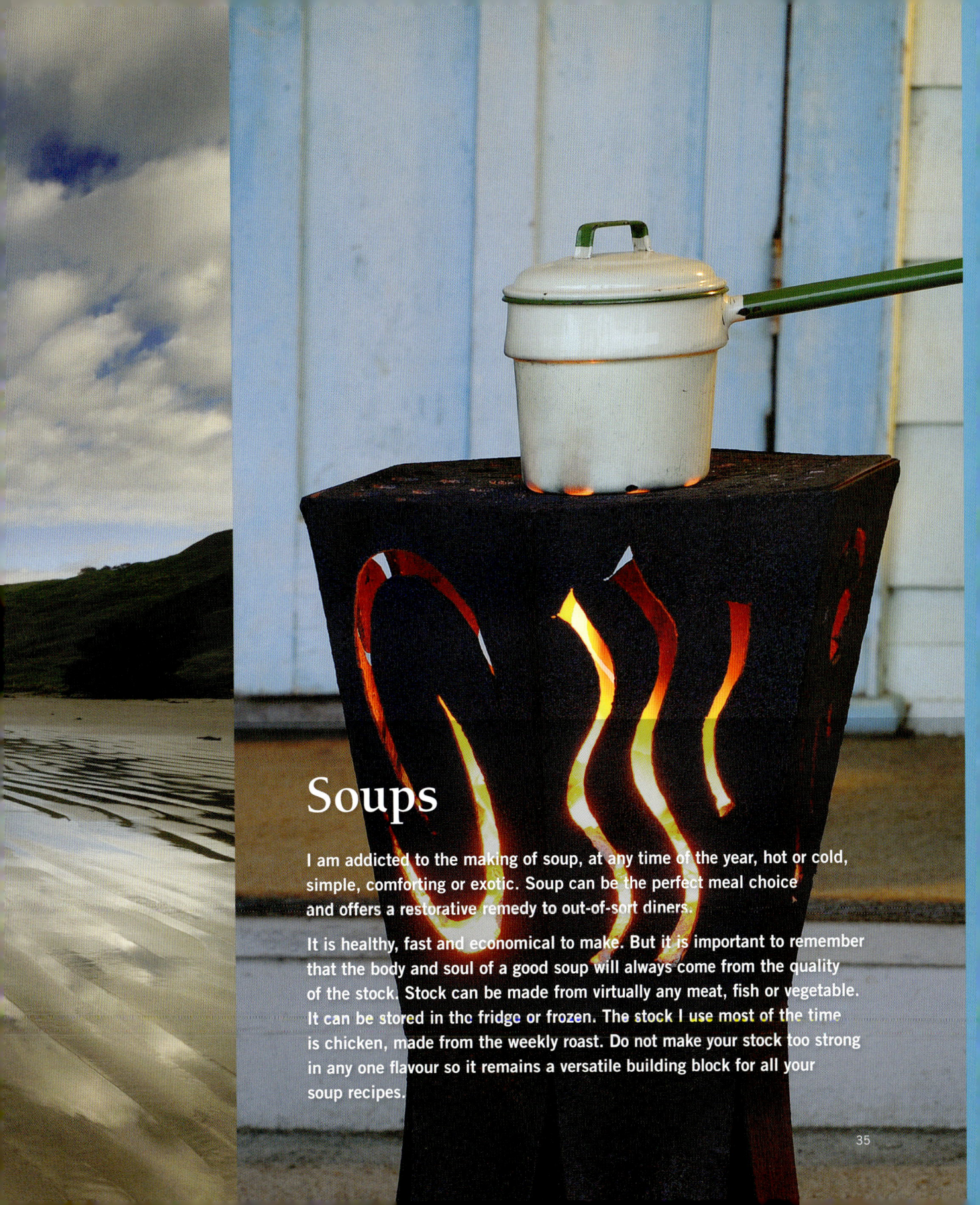

Soups

I am addicted to the making of soup, at any time of the year, hot or cold, simple, comforting or exotic. Soup can be the perfect meal choice and offers a restorative remedy to out-of-sort diners.

It is healthy, fast and economical to make. But it is important to remember that the body and soul of a good soup will always come from the quality of the stock. Stock can be made from virtually any meat, fish or vegetable. It can be stored in the fridge or frozen. The stock I use most of the time is chicken, made from the weekly roast. Do not make your stock too strong in any one flavour so it remains a versatile building block for all your soup recipes.

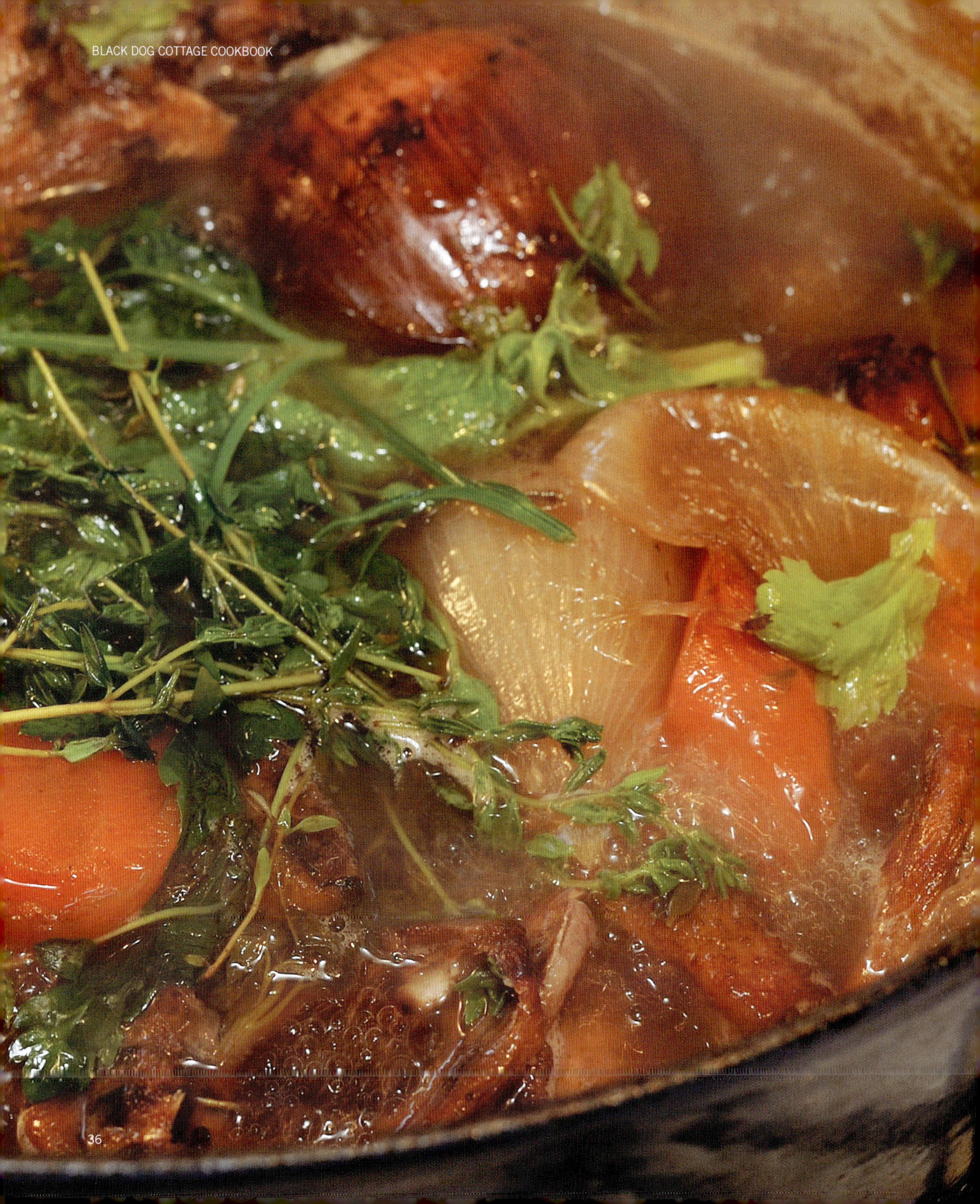

Chicken Stock

Makes approximately 1.75 litres

1 cooked chicken carcass, winglets, bones, giblets and any skin, meat and jelly
1 unpeeled onion quartered
Green part of 4 leeks, chopped
2 carrots, chopped
1 garlic clove, crushed
1 bay leaf
1 small bunch parsley
2 sprigs of thyme
6 peppercorns
A generous pinch of salt
2 litres of cold water

Method

1. Put all the ingredients in a large pan, cover with the water and bring the water slowly to the boil. Turn down the heat and let the stock simmer gently, uncovered, for two hours.
2. Drain the stock into a bowl, let it cool and then refrigerate it. Remove the layer of fat that forms on the surface before using the stock. To concentrate the flavour, reduce the chilled stock by one-third or more, depending on how intense you want the flavour to become.

When making chicken stock do so at a low simmer for at least 6 hours. This will reward you with a beautiful tasty stock. Once strained, this stock can be boiled hard and reduced to make a divine *jus*.

Thai Chicken Noodle Soup

An all-time favourite. Uncomplicated, nourishing, healthy and easy. A good pick-me-up remedy. I always make heaps because everybody adores it. To be enjoyed any time of the day.

Serves 10

1 whole chicken, legs loosely tied
2 litres light chicken stock
2 tbsp fish sauce
4 cloves garlic, left whole
1 fresh chilli, left whole
2 lemongrass stalks, cut in half, ends bashed
Bunch spring onions
Bunch coriander
1-1½ pkts dried egg noodles
(depending on how noodle-dense you want your soup to be)
50g bean sprouts
3 lettuce leaves, shredded

Method

1. Place chicken in a deep pot, pour in stock, top up with water so that chicken is just covered with liquid. Add fish sauce, garlic, chilli, lemongrass, chopped green tops of spring onions and chopped stalks and roots of the coriander bunch. Bring to the boil, turn down and simmer for 15 minutes or so. Turn off the heat, leave lid on and let chicken cool down in stock. When you come to lift out the chicken, you will find it will be perfectly cooked. Skin the chicken and shred into good size pieces, set aside. Strain the stock of all the goodies, and return stock back into your pot and reheat.
2. Add noodles and simmer for about 5 minutes adding the chopped whites of the spring onions and chopped coriander leaves at the same time (you may like to add a little chopped fresh chilli).
3. Return the chicken. Check seasoning.
4. To serve, ladle into deep bowls garnished with bean sprouts and shredded lettuce.

"The taste of good soup
holds a world of history and culture"

Claudia Roden

Lamb Harira

One-pot cooking. This hearty comfort food is even better on the second day. This is also delicious made with chicken thighs and drumsticks.

Serves 6-8

200g dried chickpeas, soaked overnight
5 lamb shanks, cut into 4
2 tbsp olive oil
2 medium onions, chopped
2 garlic cloves, chopped
1 tsp coriander seeds, roasted and ground
2 tsp cumin seeds, roasted and ground
2 tsp tumeric
1 tsp cinnamon
2 litres of vegetable stock or chicken stock or a mix
800g tomato passata
2 tbsp white wine vinegar
115g lentils, washed
115g basmati rice
5cm piece of root ginger, grated
Large bunch of coriander leaves, chopped
Bunch of flat-leaf parsley, chopped
1 lemon, juiced
Salt and pepper

Method

1. Put fresh water over the chickpeas and bring to the boil. Skim the surface, cover and lower the heat until the chickpeas are cooked. This takes about 1 hour. Drain.
2. Brown the pieces of lamb in a little oil and reserve.
3. Heat 2 tbsp of olive oil and fry the onion, garlic and spices together.
4. Add the lamb, pour over the stock, passata and vinegar. Bring to the boil, lower the heat to a gentle simmer. Cover and cook for about 30 minutes.
5. Add the lentils, simmer for another 20 minutes, then add the rice and chickpeas. Continue to bubble gently until both rice and lentils are cooked and lamb is very tender.
6. Cool overnight so that the fat rises to the top, then lift off the next day.
7. Reheat and stir in grated ginger, coriander, parsley, lemon juice, salt and pepper just before serving.

Mushroom Soup

I adore mushrooms. This soup has just the right balance of flavours. Simple and healthy.

Serves 4-6

1 large onion, chopped
1 garlic clove, crushed
2 tsp fresh thyme, chopped
350g mushrooms, chopped
1 tbsp barley
1 litre vegetable or chicken stock
1 tsp miso
Soy sauce to taste
Finely chopped fresh parsley

Method

1. Sauté onion, garlic and thyme in a little oil.
2. Add mushrooms and cook for a further few minutes.
3. Add barley and stock, bring to the boil, reduce heat, cover and simmer for 1 hour.
4. Mix in miso, soy sauce and parsley, taste and adjust seasoning.

Vegetable stocks may be boiled hard but the ingredients would have given what they are going to give within 30 minutes.

Chickpea, Leek And Roasted Tomato Soup

Simple and divine. My children adore this soup. In fact, everyone does. It's easy and rewarding. One Easter we had this at the beach for lunch, outside with the furnace going. I just put the pot on the furnace in-between helpings. A word of warning: this is not the sort of soup to have before meeting the Queen.

Serves 6

Roasted tomato sauce:

1 kg tomatoes, sliced in half
1 large brown onion, roughly chopped
1 head of garlic, cloves peeled and left whole
2 tbsp extra virgin olive oil
A few branches of thyme
1 tsp dried oregano
1 tbsp tomato paste
Salt and freshly ground pepper
Sugar to taste

Soup:

125ml extra virgin olive oil
4 leeks, white parts only, cleaned and thinly sliced
250g dried chickpeas (soaked overnight, drained and rinsed well)
6 cups light chicken stock
1 bay leaf

Method

1. Preheat oven to 200°C. Place all ingredients for the sauce into a baking dish and mix well. Roast for 40 minutes. Cool and blend in a food processor.
2. Heat olive oil in a large, heavy saucepan. Add the leeks and cook over a low heat for 10 minutes. Stir in the chickpeas and cook for another 3 minutes. Now add the stock and bay leaf. Simmer the soup for 1 hour or until the chickpeas are cooked. Stir in the roasted tomato sauce, adjust the seasoning (if necessary) and simmer for another 30 minutes.

BLACK DOG COTTAGE COOKBOOK

42   Mangakuri, dusk

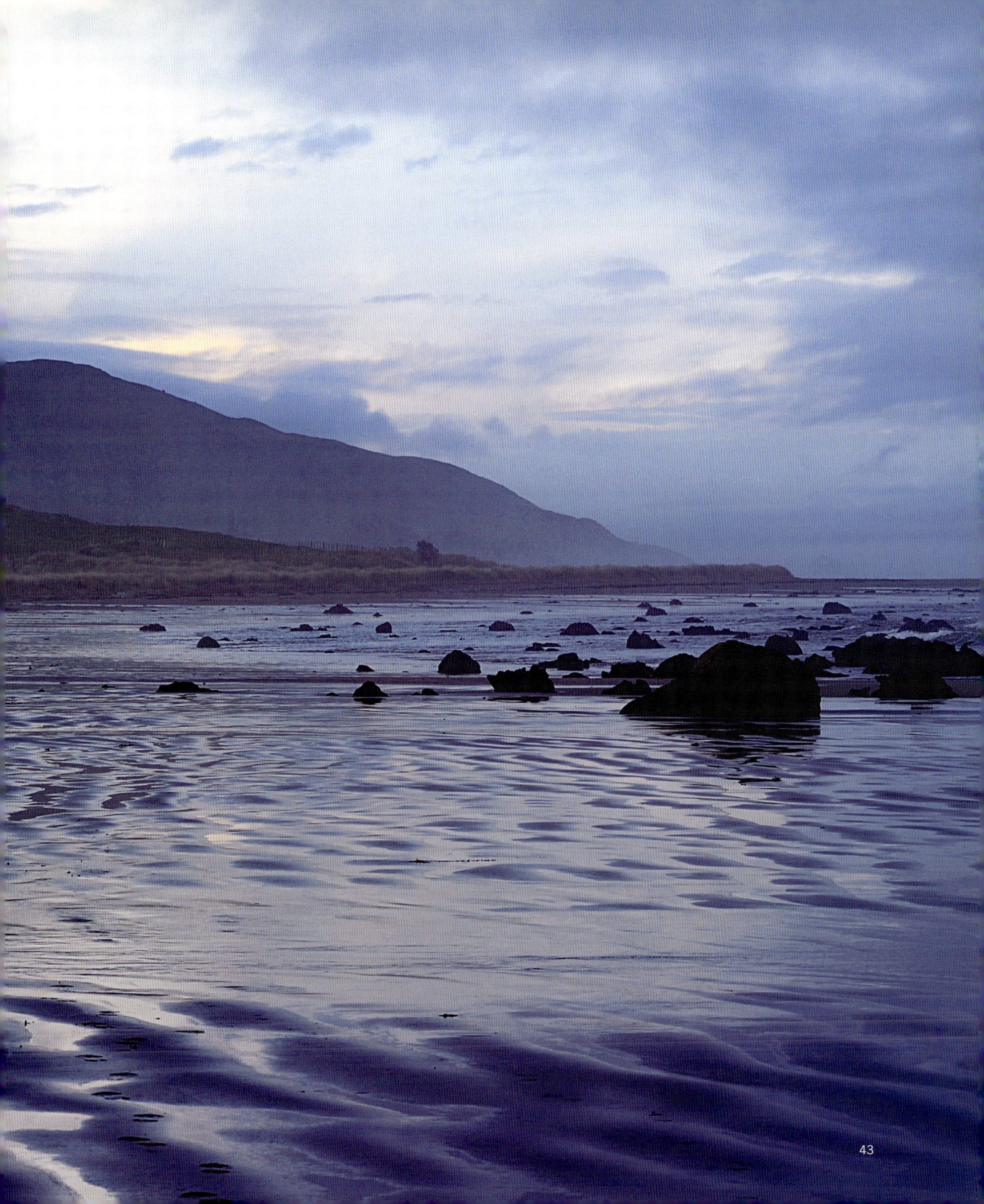

Lamb and Vegetable Barley Broth

This old-style country soup is a meal in a pot. Just like my mother used to make, it gets better as it matures. Try it around the fire with a bottle of red. Get your butcher to cut up the lamb shoulder as it is always better to cook meat on the bone. This will yield a much deeper and tastier soup. But, of course, it can also be made with a boned-out piece of lamb.

Serves 6-8

25g butter
2 tbsp oil
1 leek, chopped
2 large onions, chopped
2 garlic cloves, peeled and chopped
2 kg lamb shoulder
(left on the bone and cut into cubes)
2 carrots, peeled and chopped
2 tbsp tomato paste
2 cans Italian peeled tomatoes
1 cup barley
1-2 cups red wine
Extra stock or water to cover
Dried herbs and a bayleaf
1 parsnip, peeled and chopped
¼ pumpkin, peeled and chopped
1 kumara, peeled and chopped
2 courgettes, chopped
1 tbsp each of freshly chopped parsley and thyme

Get into the habit of making your own stock. Although there are some good ones on the shelves, they are usually over-salted. Making your own stock is unbelievably gratifying.

Method

1. Heat butter and oil together and sauté onions, leek and garlic until soft.
2. Add lamb and cook on a high heat, moving lamb around in the pot, for about 10 minutes.
3. Add carrot, paste, tomatoes, barley, wine and extra stock or water to cover meat and vegetables well.
4. Throw in a bay leaf, add salt and freshly ground pepper.
5. Cover and simmer for 60 minutes.
6. Add parsnip, pumpkin, kumara and courgettes, simmer until vegetables are done.
7. At the end of cooking, check seasoning. Finally add freshly chopped parsley and thyme.

Green Minestrone

Perfect soup for in-between seasons.

Serves 6

3 tblsp olive oil
2 garlic cloves
1 medium-sized white onion, chopped
1 fennel bulb, finely chopped
1 medium-sized carrot, finely chopped
2 celery stalks, thinly sliced
300g potatoes, finely diced
3 litres vegetable stock
2 fresh or dried bay leaves
Pinch ground cloves
Salt and freshly ground pepper
200g spaghetti, broken into 5cm lengths
2 bunches spinach, washed and shredded
500g watercress, washed and shredded
100g freshly grated or shaved parmesan cheese

Method

1. Heat oil and cook garlic, onion, fennel, carrot, celery and potatoes for 5 minutes.
2. Add stock, bay leaves, and cloves. Season. Bring to the boil. Cover and simmer for 1 hour.
3. Add spaghetti, simmer for 10 minutes.
4. Add greens, simmer for another 10 minutes.
5. Serve with shavings of parmesan.

The makings of a bouquet garni

Fish and shellfish stocks should be cooked at a bubble for no longer than 30 minutes or they may turn cloudy and bitter.

BLACK DOG COTTAGE COOKBOOK

Light Dishes

In the Mediterranean vegetables often take centre stage and meat and fish are secondary considerations when planning a meal. So it is with me. That is why this section on light dishes really represents the essence of my cooking style, they are full of colour and taste and can be used for mezzes or they can become a meal in their own right. For example, Caponata on Crostini makes a great mezze; Thai carrot salad would be a delicious side dish and Niçoise salad with Char grilled Scallops would make a lovely lunch.

These recipes are extremely versatile, simple, fresh, light and healthy combinations that are not going to take all day to prepare.

Warm Salad of New Potatoes, Cauliflower, Broccoli and Asparagus with Mint and Parsley Honey Dressing

A beautiful-looking salad as well as lovely to eat. I adore cauliflower and often eat a plate of it on its own, steamed and simply dressed with the best extra virgin olive oil I have in my pantry, a little squeeze of fresh lemon, tossed with some salt and freshly ground pepper. This dressing is a goody and is excellent with a number of things, e.g. fish, chicken, roasted beetroot or carrots and goat's cheese.

Serves 4

500g new potatoes, washed
200g cauliflower in florets
200g broccoli in florets
200g asparagus, cut into threes
100g rocket, washed and roughly chopped

Dressing:

100ml extra virgin olive oil
50ml white wine vinegar
130ml honey
2 tbsp Dijon mustard
1 dsp chopped parsley
1 dsp chopped mint
Salt and freshly ground pepper

Method

1. Steam the potatoes for 20 minutes or until they are cooked. Add them to a large bowl.
2. Steam cauliflower, broccoli and asparagus all separately until tender to the bite. Add to the bowl, then add the rocket and mix together.
3. Prepare the dressing by blending the olive oil, vinegar, honey and mustard in a food processor or a liquidizer. Taste and season.
4. Toss the vegetables in the dressing and serve at room temperature.

Briam

This has got to be one of the best and easiest baked vegetable dishes on the planet. In typical Greek style it doesn't really matter if you put in less or more of a certain vegetable. What is important, however, is that you bake it in a large flat dish, you roughly chop or slice all the vegetables, you mix everything by hand and you bake it long and slow. It is without doubt better eaten the following day at room temperature.

Serves 4 - 6

2 potatoes, peeled and sliced
1 purple onion, sliced
2 cloves of garlic, crushed
2 courgettes, sliced
1 red or green pepper, deseeded and sliced
1 aubergine, halved, chopped into chunks
5 medium sized tomatoes, roughly chopped
120ml extra virgin olive oil
120g tomato paste mixed with 350mls of warm water
Salt and freshly ground pepper
Handful of dill, roughly chopped

Method

1. Pre-heat oven to 150°C.
2. Put all the chopped and sliced vegetables into your baking dish. It does not matter in what order, there is no order to this dish. Pour over the oil, the tomato paste mixed with water, season and scatter over the dill. Do not worry if it doesn't seem enough liquid to bake all the vegetables, remember that the raw tomatoes will render their own liquid.
3. Mix everything with your hands and baked uncovered for at least 1½ hours, turning over once or twice.
4. The next day, check seasoning and freshen with a little more dill.

"After a good dinner one can forgive anybody, even one's own relatives"
Oscar Wilde

Puy Lentils with Sautéed Vegetables

Top these lentils with fish, chicken or lamb as I have done here in the photograph with roasted salmon and finished off with pea sauce (see *Essentials*). Or serve with salad leaves and maybe some goat's cheese. There's something about lentils and lettuce leaves, they combine beautifully together. Lentils will keep fresh in your refrigerator for at least four days.

Serves 4

350g puy lentils

750ml water

2 bay leaves

1-2 tsp olive oil

125g shallots, finely chopped plus 1 left whole

2 cloves garlic, chopped

1 carrot, finely chopped, plus 1 whole

1 bunch of spring onions, finely chopped

1 red pepper, finely chopped

Bunch of fresh coriander, chopped

Salt and pepper

A good glug of your best olive oil

A splash of your best balsamic vinegar

Method

1. To cook the lentils, wash them, put them in a pot and cover with water. Throw in a halved shallot, a halved carrot, 2 bay leaves, and the stalks and roots of the coriander. Bring to the boil, cover and simmer until cooked for about 20 minutes. Check to see if they are cooked by biting into them. They should be al dente. Cook for a little longer if need be. Drain and lift out bay leaves, carrots, etc.
2. While the lentils are cooking, heat the olive oil and add chopped shallots, garlic, carrots, spring onions, and peppers. Sauté until all is softened. I quite like having the vegetables still a little crunchy, but this is up to you. Add the vegetables to the lentils along with seasoning, coriander, and a fresh glug of olive oil and balsamic vinegar. Taste and adjust seasoning to your liking.

Lentils: I tend to use the puy lentil (which is black), or the little organic brown lentil. They hold their shape, don't turn to mush and their taste is superior to other lentils. If you have a packet of these in your pantry, you can make a meal on a whim. Remember to dress them while they are still warm so they absorb all the flavours. Most importantly, don't salt them while they are cooking as this hardens the lentil. They are an excellent base for any fish, chicken or meat dish.

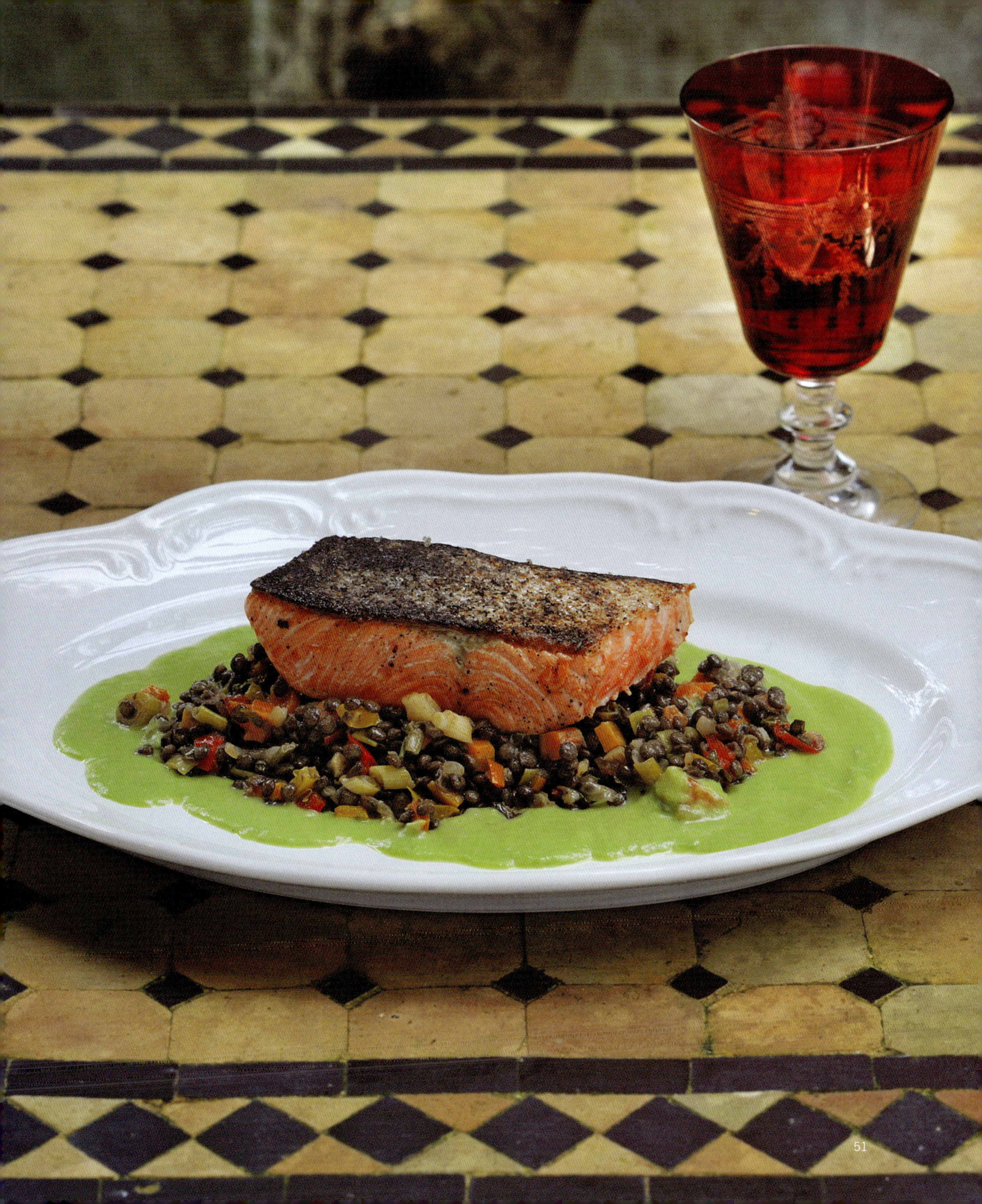

Grilled Vegetable and Pasta Salad with Lemon Mustard Dressing

My husband Mattie and I used to make this together, at the beach. It was his job to char-grill all the vegetables. We always had such fun making and then eating the salad together – with a glass of wine, looking out to sea. This dressing is excellent with salad, vegetables, chicken or fish and can be stored in the refrigerator, in a sealed jar for up to a week.

Serves 4

Choose a variety of vegetables in season, e.g. asparagus
1 pepper
Zucchini
Red onions
Aubergine
Tomatoes, halved and seeded
1 cup chopped fresh basil or oregano
½ cup chopped fresh flat parsley
Salt and pepper
Lemon mustard dressing
Penne pasta, cooked al dente

Lemon Mustard Dressing

6 cloves garlic, crushed
½ tsp salt
3-4 tblsp Dijon mustard
3 tbsp fresh lemon juice
4 tblsp olive oil
Ground black pepper
Cayenne pepper to taste

Method

1. Oil vegetables and chargrill.
2. Cut into uneven, bite-sized pieces.
3. Toss vegetables with pasta.
4. Combine all the ingredients for the dressing together and beat well. Toss some of the lemon mustard dressing along with the chopped herbs through the pasta and vegetables. Leave overnight if possible.
5. Bring salad up to room temperature before serving, adding a little more dressing if necessary.

Aubergines are at their best in late summer and autumn. Pick aubergines that are heavy and firm with glossy skins. I prefer to use the long elongated ones when they are around. They never seem to have any bitterness to them. Just be careful that they are not too seedy.

Thai Carrot Salad

My friend Annabel Graham introduced me to this salad when I worked with her at the Dunsandel Store. It is my kind of food, less is more. Winter or summer. Eat this any time, anywhere. Pleasing on the eye, yummy and goes with everything. A must-have for your repertoire. If you make it beforehand, just dress it a little to let the flavours mingle and become acquainted. Refresh with extra dressing before serving. The carrot will only absorb so much so if you overdress it, you will end up with a very wet salad. Children love this salad as well.

Serves 4

4 large carrots, grated in the food processor
1 red capsicum, julienned
1 bunch spring onions, julienned
1 bunch coriander, chopped
1 bunch mint, chopped
Handful peanuts, dry fried and chopped
1-2 tbsp toasted sesame seeds for garnish

Dressing:

3 tbsp grapeseed oil
1 tbsp rice vinegar
2 tsp fish sauce

Method

Put all the salad ingredients in a large bowl. Pour over the dressing, don't make it too wet. Tip out onto a large flat plate and garnish with toasted sesame seeds.

The addition of a freshly chopped herb at the end of your finished dish will add an interesting, balanced and calculated twist to the end result.

Rocket and Feta Tortilla

Tortillas are perfect for lunch, a picnic, a light dinner or cut into small squares to have with a drink. Of course you can add anything you fancy to a tortilla, but remember to keep it simple. They are often the best combinations, rather than complicated ones. This recipe is a fine example of just that.

Serves 6

1 tbsp extra virgin olive oil
1 clove garlic, crushed
1 onion, chopped
100gm feta
1 bunch rocket
250gm potatoes (parboiled), chopped
6 eggs
⅓ cup cream
1 lemon, zest
Salt and freshly ground pepper
Grated cheese to lightly cover

Method

1. Pre-heat oven to 180°C.
2. Heat the oil and sauté the garlic and onion, add the potatoes and crisp a little.
3. Beat eggs and cream lightly, break in the feta cheese and add the chopped rocket, zest, salt and pepper and pour over the potatoes. Top with grated cheese and bake for 15 minutes.
4. Serve hot or cold cut into wedges.

Shitake and Celery Heart Salad with Muscatels and Walnuts

Justin North introduced me to this combination. It is a fabulous tasty salad either on its own or with duck, venison or beef. I often make this around Christmas time, but it's just as good in the depths of winter.

Serves 4

100g shitake mushrooms, finely sliced
70g oyster mushrooms, finely sliced
1 head of celery
(golden heart and leaves only)
½ cup roasted walnuts
½ cup muscatels

For the walnut vinaigrette:

2 tsp Dijon mustard
30ml sherry vinegar
2 roasted walnuts
Salt and pepper to taste
70ml walnut oil
60ml grapeseed oil

Method

1. For the salad: pick the lime green leaves from the celery, peel and finely slice the golden heart and mix with the finely sliced raw shitake and oyster mushrooms, roasted walnuts and muscatels. Drizzle with a little of the walnut vinaigrette and toss together.
2. For the walnut vinaigrette: place the mustard, vinegar, nuts and seasoning in a mortar and pound to a coarse paste (or use a food processor). Slowly add the oils, whisking constantly. Taste and adjust the seasoning to your liking.

BLACK DOG COTTAGE COOKBOOK

Warm Sweet Corn Salad

Beautiful vegetable dish when corn is at its peak. Great at room temperature. Sometimes I leave the feta out and I often use just what herbs I have on hand.

A handy hint: When I'm taking the corn off the cob, I stand the cob actually in the sautéing pan with the onion, spring onion, and chilli. That way the corn doesn't go everywhere and falls directly into the pan.

Serves 4-5

2 tbsp extra virgin olive oil
1 onion, chopped
1 red chilli, seeds removed and chopped
Bunch spring onions, chopped
4 fresh corn cobs, kernels removed
1 bunch of coriander, basil, and chives
1 packet mild feta, broken into chunks
Salt and pepper

Method

1. Heat 1 tbsp of the oil in a large flat pan. When hot add onion, chilli, and spring onions. Soften a little then add the corn. Keep cooking this until the corn is just beginning to change colour, i.e. to a deeper yellow and has lost that slightly floury taste. This will probably take no more than 10 minutes, depending on how fresh the corn is.
2. When it has cooled a little, add the herbs, remaining oil, broken feta, salt and freshly ground pepper.

Warm salads are meals in themselves, perfect for a lunch or a light supper. They are fun to create, nourishing and satisfying, both on the eye and the stomach. A warm salad is my preferred way of eating, as every component is honest, clean and unadulterated.

Thai Noodle Salad

One of the very first things I ever taught and to this day it remains a firm favourite.

Serves 4
500g spaghetti
Julienne of carrot or any vegetable mixture you choose

Dressing
½ cup each of basil, coriander and mint
Chilli, seeds removed
2 tbsp soya
⅓ cup fish sauce
Juice of 2 limes
¾ cup olive oil

Method
1. Chop herbs roughly. Place in blender.
2. Add chilli, soya, fish sauce and lime juice.
3. Slowly add olive oil.
4. Pour dressing over warm noodles and julienne of vegetables.

I mix salads with my hands, as this is the only way every leaf will be properly covered in the dressing.

Caponata

Divine. Colourful caponata is the Italian ratatouille. Perfect as a base, as a drink snack with crostini, for lunch, at room temperature. Enjoy all the different layers of taste. I like to cut all the vegetables into small dice, but this is optional. It gets better if it's left to sit and the flavours are able to get acquainted. The sugar and vinegar gives it a sweet/sour note and the addition of anchovies and black olives give it a strength that other caponata recipes just don't have.

I use anchovies to bring out the other flavours in the dish, not to take over whatever I am using them with.

Serves 6 (as a main)
3 eggplants
Salt
Extra virgin olive oil
3 red peppers
1 large onion
½ heart celery, or 2 celery stalks
30g sugar
100g tomato paste
100ml vinegar
Chopped parsley
25g capers
50g black olives (pitted and halved)
2 anchovies, drained and chopped
60g sultanas
50g pinenuts

Method
1. Peel and cut eggplant into cubes. Cover the bottom of your pan with olive oil and heat to very hot. Throw in batches of aubergine (do not overcrowd the pan). Sauté until soft. Lift out and repeat until all the aubergine is done.
2. Grill peppers, peel and chop into dice.
3. Dice the celery and onion. Heat another good glug of oil and sauté until limp.
4. Add sugar, vinegar and tomato paste and cook for a few minutes.
5. Add the parsley, capers, olives, chopped anchovies, eggplant, prepared peppers, sultanas and pinenuts.
6. Gently simmer for about 5 minutes. Then leave these flavours to marry together, overnight if possible.
7. Bring to room temperature before serving or heat ever so gently.

Cannellini Bean, Corn and Fresh Herb Salad

Marvellous on its own or as a base under fish, crayfish or lamb as it is here in the photograph, surrounded by a fresh tomato concassé and finished off with a dollop of aioli and lemon pickle (see *Essentials* for these recipes). Winter or summer, warm or cold, it is a beautiful salad or vegetable dish.

Serves 4

300g cannellini beans, soaked overnight
1 ½ lemons, juiced
100ml extra virgin olive oil
1 bunch of spring onions, sliced (green part as well)
2-3 cobs of corn, steamed and kernels taken off the cob
2 tbsp snipped chives
2 tbsp chopped basil
Salt and freshly ground pepper

Method

1. Drain beans. Place beans in a large pot and cover with lots of water (do not salt). Bring to the boil. Cover and simmer for about 20 minutes. They may need a little longer or a little less, this depends on the freshness of the beans. When tender to the bite, drain and pour over lemon juice and olive oil.
2. Throw in spring onions, corn, herbs, and seasoning.
3. You may need to add extra oil/lemon and seasoning.

Flavour your food with fresh herbs. Use them instead of salt. Add them at the end of cooking, so they remain fresh and green in the finished dish.

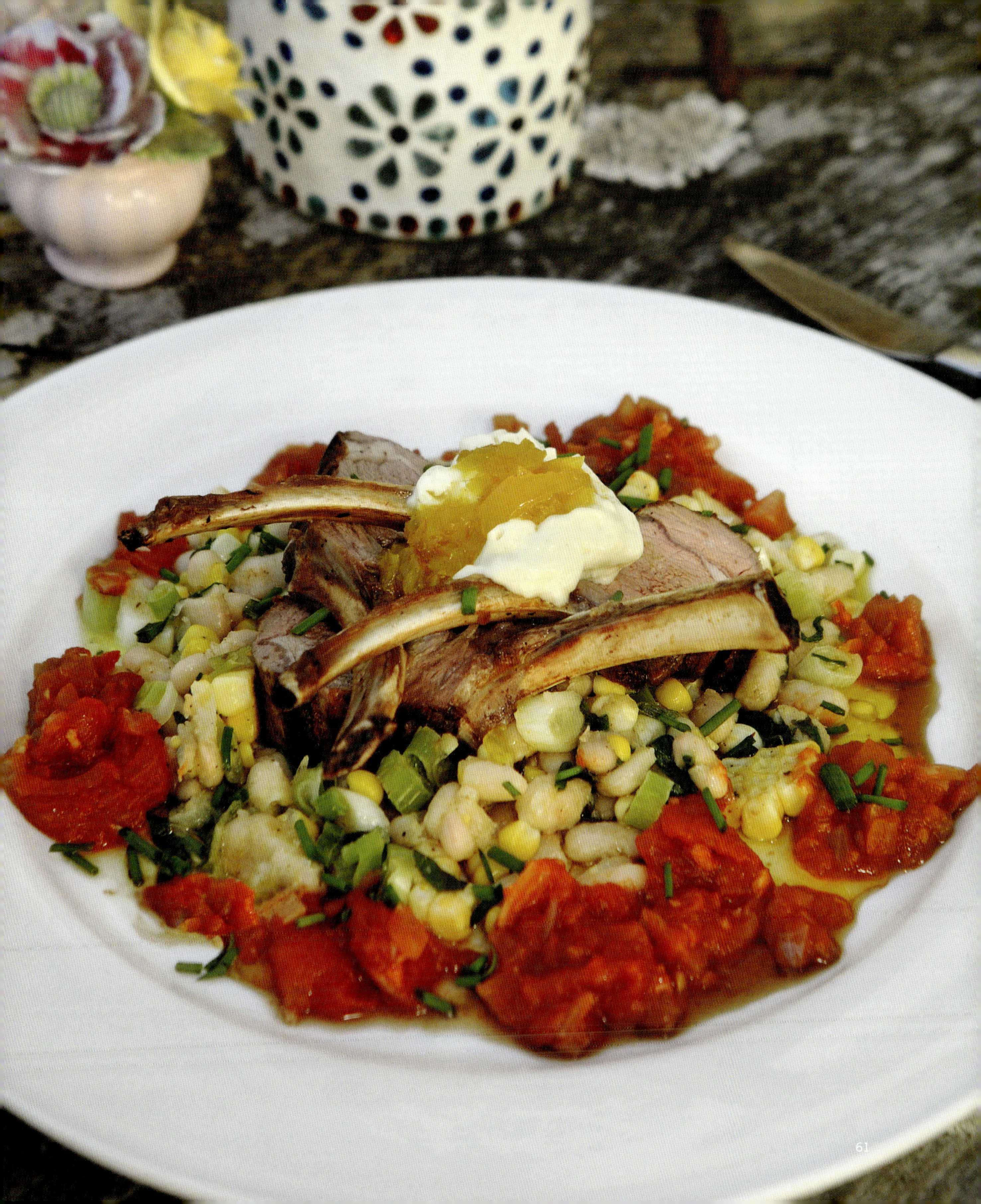

BLACK DOG COTTAGE COOKBOOK

The bach

Giant Baked Beans with Tomatoes and Dill

One of those gorgeous dishes that reminds me so much of Greece. Beautiful on its own and great with lamb, or fish. I like to glaze these beans with a good glug of my very best extra virgin olive oil before serving. Also, some crusty fresh bread that you can drag through the beans never goes amiss either.

Serves 8

400g large lima beans, soaked overnight
100 ml extra virgin olive oil
2 onions, thinly sliced
2 carrots, peeled and finely chopped
1 stalk celery, finely chopped
4 cloves garlic, finely chopped
500g tomatoes, peeled, seeded and finely chopped
1 400g can chopped tomatoes
1 tbsp tomato paste
1 tbsp dried oregano
1 tsp honey
1 small bunch of fresh dill, finely chopped
Salt and freshly ground black pepper
Extra virgin oil for glazing, optional

Method

1. Drain beans, refresh and place beans in saucepan. Cover well with cold water and bring to the boil. Simmer for 1 hour. Drain two-thirds of a cup of cooling liquid and reserve.
2. Preheat oven to 160°C.
3. Heat oil and sauté onions, carrots and celery for 20 minutes. Add garlic, tomatoes, canned tomatoes, tomato paste, oregano, honey, dill, beans, reserved liquid, salt and pepper. Cook for a few minutes, stirring constantly.
4. Place mixture in a baking dish and bake for about 1½ hours, until beans are soft and most of the liquid has evaporated.

Niçoise Salad Sauce

The marvellous thing about this sauce is that there is no cooking – just a bit of chopping, then you mix the ingredients together. I like to keep everything on the smallish side but it's up to you. It's perfect with seafood, fish, meat or anything char-grilled. It has a certain sharpness to it that cuts through the oiliness of char-grilled food. Remember to check the balance of flavours after it has sat for 30 minutes or so; you may want to make some adjustments.

Serves 2

1 anchovy fillet, finely chopped
1½ tbsp red wine vinegar
10 kalamata olives, pitted and quartered
2 tsp capers, roughly chopped
2 tbsp mixed sweet peppers, seeded and cut into dice
1 tbsp finely cut flat parsley
2 tbsp finely chopped spring onions
2 tbsp extra virgin olive oil

Method

Mix all together, and season to taste with salt and pepper.

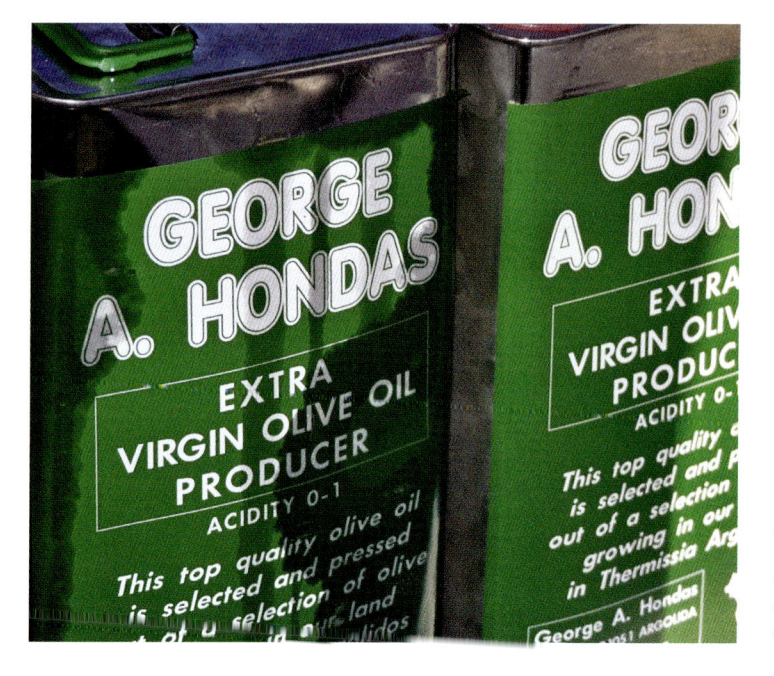

Take the time to prepare dressings or vinaigrettes. They transform your salad to another level and it never goes without being noticed.

65

BLACK DOG COTTAGE COOKBOOK

My kitchen in Wellington

'Greeky' Aubergine, Coriander and Roasted Walnut Salad

Easy tasty salads are always appreciated. You could make this with asparagus when it is in season. Use pinenuts instead of walnuts.

Serves 4-6

1 kg aubergine, the thin Asian-type ones, if they are in season
55g walnuts
1 bunch spring onions, finely chopped
2 garlic cloves, very finely chopped
4 tbsp extra virgin olive oil
4 tsp lemon juice
Salt and pepper to taste
1 bunch coriander, finely chopped
1 large shallot, very finely chopped

Method

1. Slice aubergines in half, lightly oil and grill on the barbecue until charred and soft. When cool enough to handle, chop into bite-size chunks and place in a bowl.
2. Add spring onions, garlic, coriander and shallots to the bowl.
3. Roast walnuts and tip into bowl.
4. Whisk the olive oil, lemon juice and seasoning together and pour over salad.

Aubergines, tomatoes, peppers and courgettes are all at their best at the same time. That is late summer and into the autumn. What a happy coincidence, especially for someone who enjoys a Mediterranean bent to their cooking. Autumn is my favourite season.

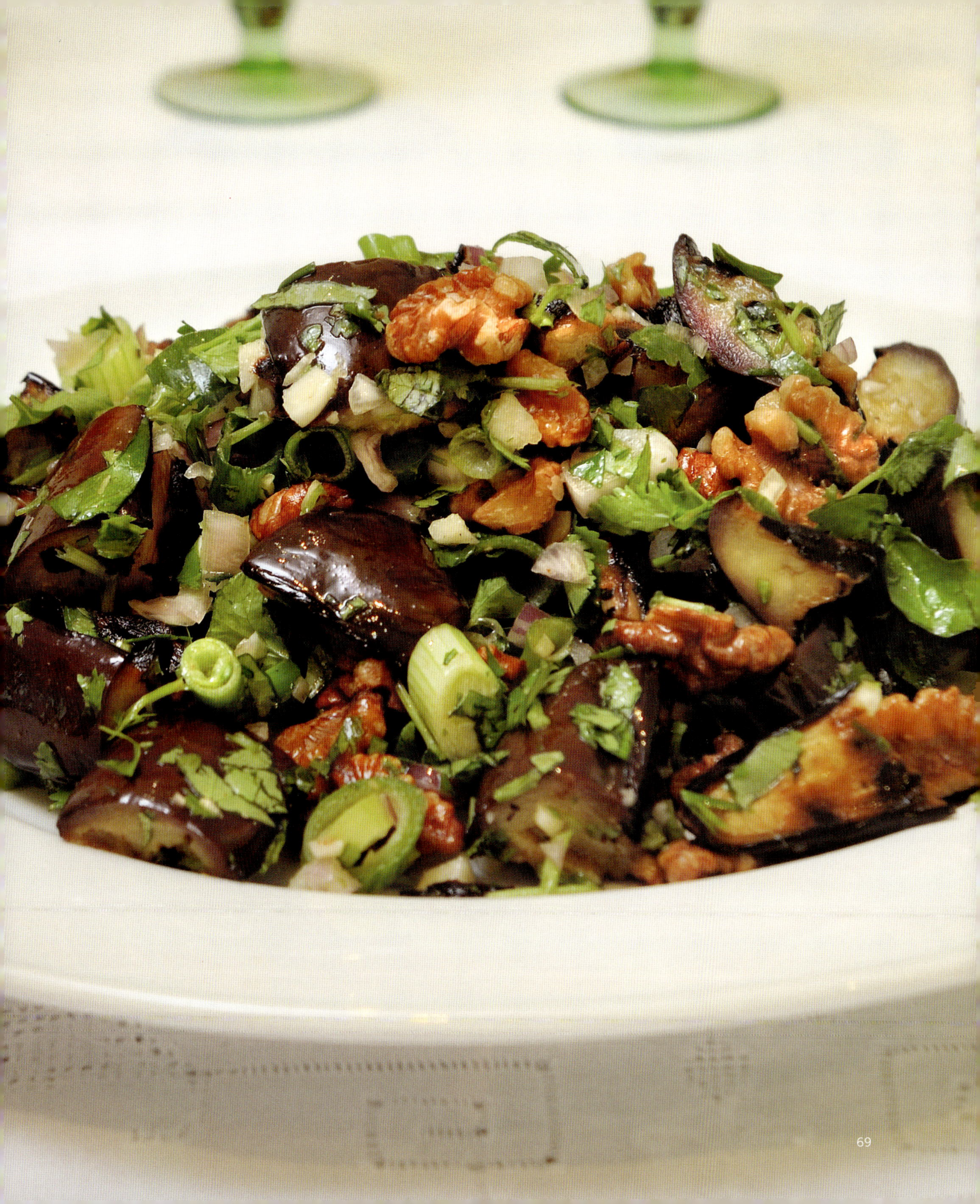

BLACK DOG COTTAGE COOKBOOK

Celeriac Rémoulade

Celeriac is a fabulous vegetable chopped, mashed, in soups or made into chips. This rémoulade is delicious with a piece of salmon, rare beef, or chicken on top.

Serves 4

500g of celeriac root, peeled and grated

2 tbsp lemon juice

Salt and freshly ground pepper

¼ pint mayonnaise, use Aioli recipe without the garlic (see *Essentials*)

1 tbsp Dijon mustard

1 tsp white wine vinegar

2 small gherkins

1 tbsp finely chopped parsley

1 tbsp snipped chives

1 dsp capers

Method

1. Make your mayonnaise as usual, then flavour with the mustard, vinegar, gherkins, parsley, chives and capers.
2. Bring some slightly lemon-infused water to the boil and tip in the grated celeriac. Blanch for 1-2 minutes. Drain well and squeeze out any excess moisture with your hands, then spread the celeriac on a tea-cloth, and pat dry.
3. Adjust the seasoning of the mayonnaise which should be quite piquant and peppery. Stir in the celeriac until well coated all over with the mayonnaise. Chill for at least 15 minutes, or longer.

Broad Bean, Pea, Asparagus, Spring Onion and Herbs

This is one of my all-time favourite vegetable dishes, which is a visual treat as well as being divine to eat. Use it as a base for any fish, chicken or meat dish. It can be made in advance, but just be careful not to 'cook' it again when you heat it up, as you will lose the beautiful green colours. I nearly always surround the dish with a fresh tomato concassé (see *Essentials*). Serve it for lunch, or for a vegetarian course with gorgeous big chunks of your favourite goat's cheese flicked through it.

Serves 6

1 onion, finely chopped
1 bunch spring onions, chopped
2 cloves garlic, finely chopped
2 bunches asparagus, steamed and each stalk chopped into three
500g broad beans, frozen or fresh, steamed and skins removed
250g peas, fresh or frozen
1 bunch parsley, chopped
Handful of snipped chives
Handful of basil, chopped
Large dollop of butter
Salt and pepper

Method

1. Heat a glug of extra virgin olive oil in a large skillet, add the onion, spring onions and garlic. Cook gently over a medium heat until soft, do not let the mixture brown.
2. Add the peas, cook for 5 minutes. Add asparagus and broad beans, cook for a further 5 minutes.
3. Add all the herbs, season and finish with a good dollop of butter.

"Less is more"

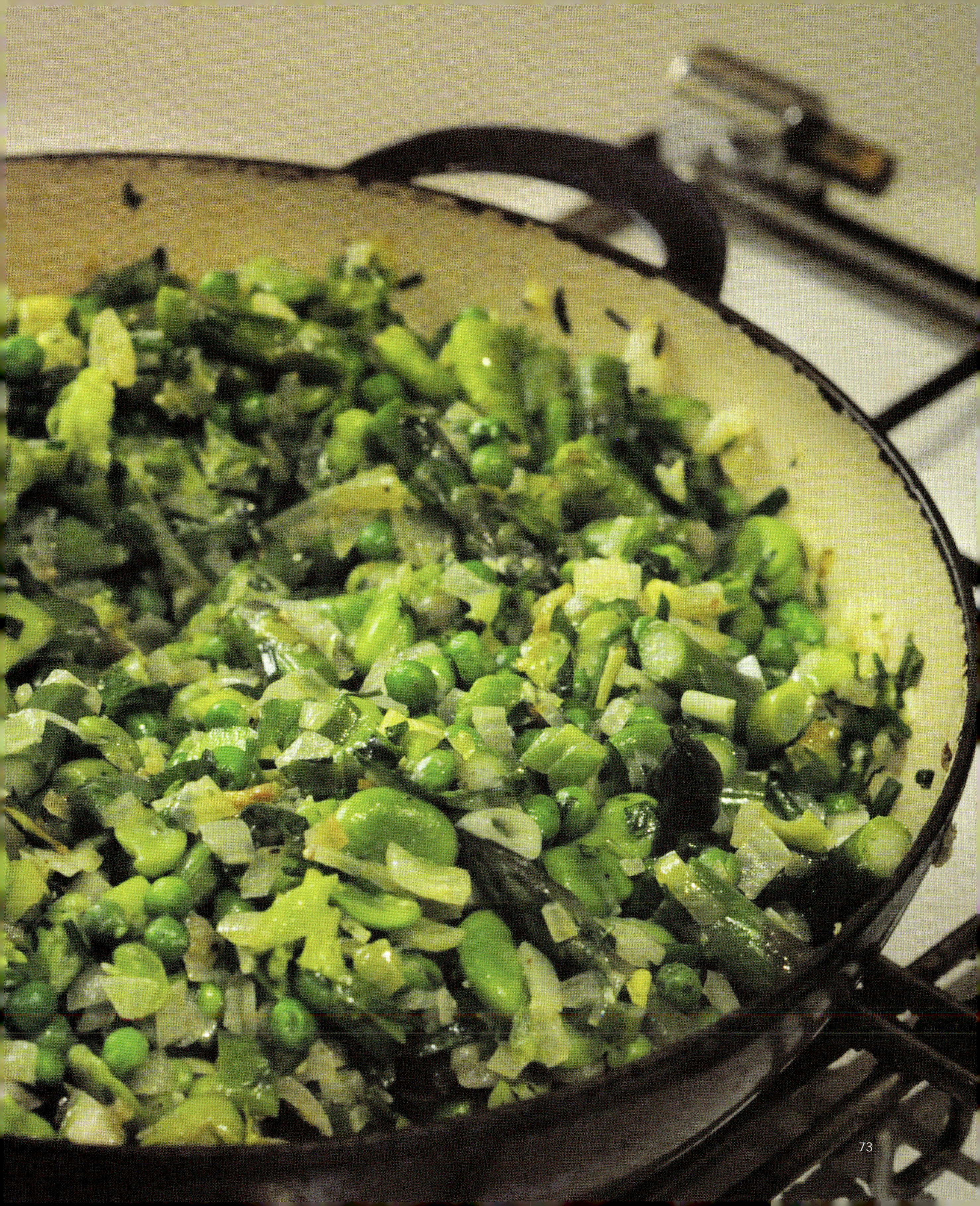

Hydra Salad

We would order this green salad with every meal on Hydra. So incredibly simple, and yet so utterly divine.

1 cos lettuce
1 clove of garlic
1 bunch spring onions
½ packet dill
Extra virgin olive oil
½ lemon

Method

1. Slice cos roughly, place on plate. Crush clove of garlic over lettuce. Chop spring onions and dill and throw on top. Get the best extra virgin olive oil you have in your pantry and sprinkle over lettuce, spring onions and dill. Season with Maldon salt and freshly ground pepper. Place half a lemon on the side ready for you to squeeze and to finish off this perfect green salad.

Simplicity will always outshine the more complicated or elaborate food.

Sumac-spiced Tuna Salad

Sumac is a wonderful sour Middle Eastern spice; ground from dark red berries, it adds a real tang to tuna, salmon or swordfish. If you cannot find it, use ground lightly roasted cumin seeds instead.

Serves 4

2 small Lebanese cucumbers, peeled, halved lengthways
2 vine-ripened tomatoes, halved
½ red capsicum, seeds removed, roughly chopped
4 small radishes, sliced
6 spring onions, sliced
5 tbsp roughly chopped flat leaf parsley
3 tbsp roughly chopped mint
1 tbsp ground sumac
4 small tuna steaks or swordfish
Salt and freshly ground pepper
1 dstp extra virgin olive oil

For the dressing:

¼ cup (60ml) olive oil
2 tbsp lemon juice
1 garlic clove, crushed
1 tsp ground cinnamon
1 tbsp ground sumac

Method

1. Scoop out and discard the seeds from the cucumber. Scoop out and discard the seeds and juice from the tomatoes.
2. Chop the cucumber, tomatoes and capsicum and mix with the radishes, spring onions, parsley and mint.
3. To make the dressing, whisk together the olive oil, lemon juice, garlic, cinnamon and sumac. Season with salt and freshly ground pepper.
4. For the fish, mix additional sumac with sea salt and freshly ground black pepper on a plate, and press one side of the tuna into it. Heat the oil in a fry pan and sear tuna, spice-side down, for 2 minutes then turn to briefly cook the other side for one minute, leaving centre pink. Remove, cover and rest for at least 5 minutes, then cut into large chunks.
5. Toss salad and tuna in the dressing and serve immediately.

Rosti with Pastry Topping

This flavour combination is to die for. Quick and easy. Divine for lunch with a salad.

Serves 4
1 large leek
1 tbsp butter
100g mushrooms
Salt and pepper
Freshly grated nutmeg
1 tsp wine (white)
100g double cream
2-3 large potatoes, peeled
1 tsp finely chopped parsley
1 tsp finely chopped chervil
4 tbsp clarified butter

For the topping:
150g puff pastry
1 egg yolk, lightly beaten to glaze

Method
1. Cut leek into julienne and fry gently in butter. Add mushrooms and cook briefly. Season with salt and pepper and nutmeg. Add white wine and stir in double cream and bring to the boil.
2. Coarsely grate potatoes and add herbs and season.
3. Melt clarified butter in a large ovenproof frying pan, sprinkle in the potatoes, pat into a 'pancake' and fry on both sides until golden brown.
4. For the topping, roll out pastry as thinly as possible. Drain off any excess fat from potatoes, leaving them in the pan.
5. Cover the leek and mushroom mixture with pastry. Glaze with beaten egg.
6. Place in oven, pre-heated to 220°C, and bake for 10-15 minutes or until the pastry is golden and puffed. Leave to rest for about 5 minutes before you slice it into wedges.

77 Mangakuri

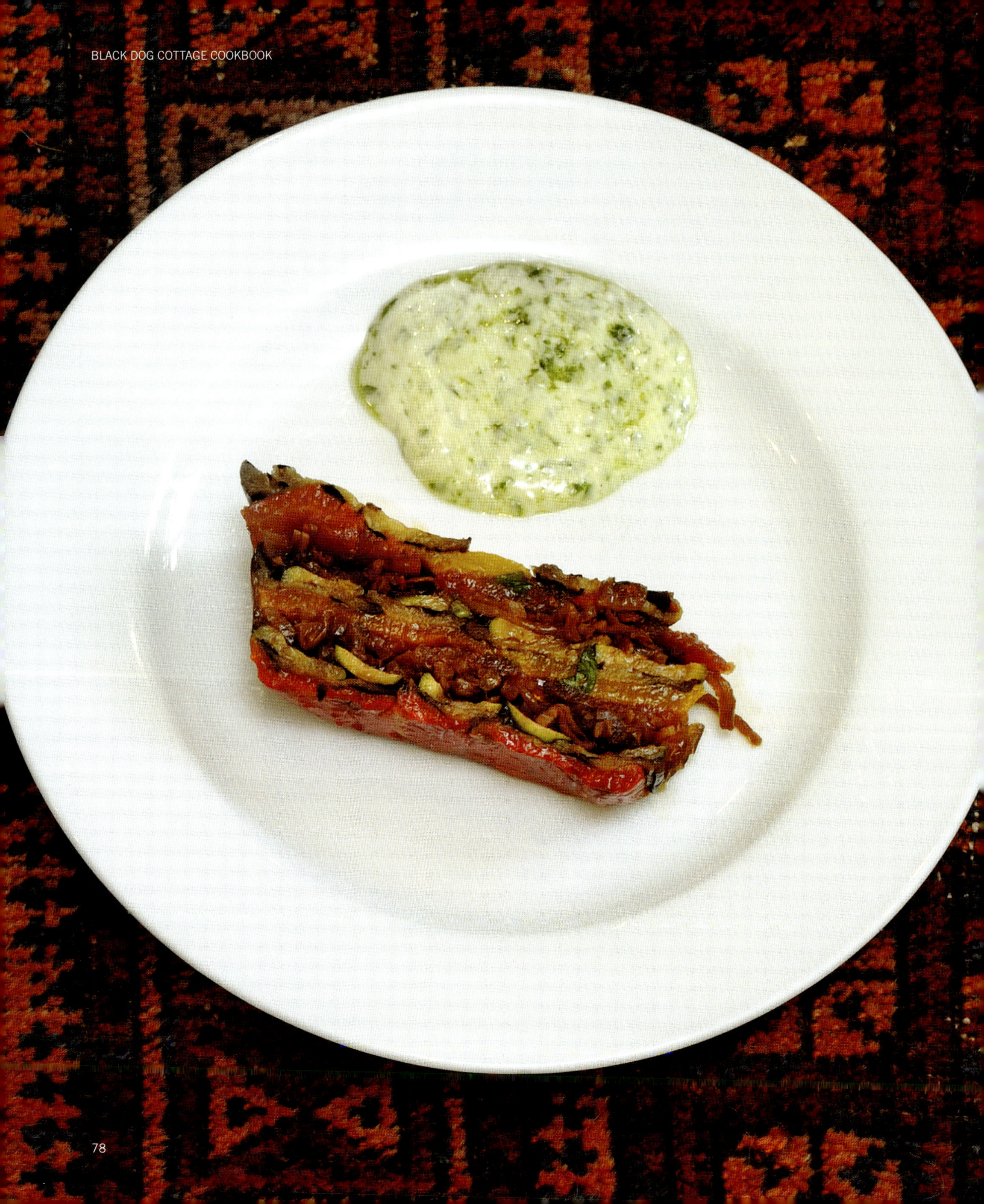

Mediterranean Vegetable Terrine

I love terrines with all their layers of taste and colour, and this one is no exception. Take your time over the preparation, I usually do it over two days. The great thing about terrines is they tend to go a long way and remain fresh and tasty for a few days. Serve with a dollop of aioli (see *Essentials*), perhaps flavoured with some basil.

Serves 12

- 1 Le Creuset cast-iron terrine or a loaf tin
- 4 large red capsicums
- 4 large yellow capsicums
- 2 long eggplant
- 4 long zucchini
- Virgin olive oil for cooking
- 3 red Spanish onions, cut into fine rings
- 1 cup loosely packed dried raisins
- 2 tbsp tomato paste
- 2 tbsp balsamic vinegar
- 4 large firm red tomatoes
- ½ bunch basil
- 3 leaves gelatine
- Maldon salt
- Freshly ground black pepper
- Finely snipped fresh marjoram

Method

1. Grill the peppers until blackened and blistered. Cool, remove skins, reserve the juices. Divide into 2 or 3 pieces.
2. Slice eggplant and zucchini lengthwise. Brush eggplant and zucchini with a little olive oil and grill.
3. Throw a nice healthy glug of oil into a pan and sauté onion rings with raisins, tomato paste and balsamic vinegar over a very low heat until caramelized and golden. This will take about 30 minutes.
4. Peel tomatoes, slice in half and remove seeds.
5. To assemble the terrine: line the terrine with some cling film, for easy turn-out, then begin with a layer of red capsicum and continue layering in the following sequence: eggplant, zucchini, onion/raisin marmalade, tomato halves, basil, finishing with yellow capsicum. Season with salt, freshly ground pepper and finely snipped fresh marjoram. Reserve all the juices.
6. Soak sheets of gelatine in cold water. Squeeze. Boil reserved juices and dissolve the gelatine. Pour into terrine and set in refrigerator overnight.
7. To serve, unmold onto a carving board and slice, using a very sharp knife.

BLACK DOG COTTAGE COOKBOOK

Family & Friends

This section is about sharing and cooking food with a generous spirit. Most importantly you don't have to buy expensive ingredients – it's time and love that are the most precious ingredients in home cooking.

These recipes focus on preparation, planning and delivery. The essential mise en place means that most of the meal is prepared in advance. Last minute preparations are minimal and getting food to the table is stress-free.

Although restaurant food certainly has an impact on the food we cook, home cooking is not restaurant food. It must be something you enjoy to cook as well as eating.

Good food does not have to be fancy. Cooking for family and friends is what it's all about for me. The following recipes have been cooked and enjoyed around our table with our children, with their friends and ours.

Philly's Fish Pie

My mother-in-law, Philly, gave me this recipe when I was desperate to get my children to eat some fish and you know what – it worked! I always put potato chips on the top for them.

Serves 6-8

800g fresh fish fillets like terakihi
1 tbsp butter
Glug oil
1 onion, finely chopped
2 sticks celery, finely chopped
2 cloves garlic, finely chopped
2 large mushrooms, chopped
1 dsp capers
1 tbsp parsley, finely chopped

Bechamel Sauce:

55g butter
55g flour
575ml milk
Yolks of 3 eggs
40g grated Parmesan (optional)

Topping Choices:

Breadcrumbs, mixed with a little grated cheese
Potato chips
Potato mash
Sliced cooked potatoes

Family cat, Dora.

Method

1. Cut the fillets into large chunks, dry on kitchen paper towel and sear quickly in a little ghee. Set aside.
2. Melt butter and oil together, gently fry the onion, celery and garlic. After about 5 minutes, add the mushrooms. Cook for another 2 minutes or so then add your capers and parsley. Check seasoning.
3. Make bechamel sauce: Melt the butter in a saucepan over a low heat. Stir in the flour and cook for about 3 minutes. Whisk in the milk. Simmer for 5-10 minutes. Beat in the eggs and then the cheese if you wish. Reserve. Now combine the celery/mushroom mixture with some of the bechamel sauce and the fish pieces.
4. Place into a pie dish, and top with reserved bechamel sauce and desired topping. Place in a pre-heated 180°C oven for approximately 15 minutes.

Fried Noodles with Chicken and Shrimps

Fabulous! Everyone loves this wok dish, so be sure you make enough. It's one of those dishes that keep you going back for 'just a little more'.

Serves 4

1 egg
2 small green chillies
About 4 tbsp fish sauce
2 garlic cloves
3 small shallots
3 tbsp dried shrimps, soaked in warm water for 10 minutes and drained
3 tbsp peanut oil
150g chicken breasts, thinly sliced
3 tbsp sambal olek (optional)
350g thin egg noodles, cooked and drained
2 bok choy, thinly sliced
150g cooked shrimps
25g Chinese (garlic) chives
4 iceberg lettuce leaves, rolled and shredded
30g crispy red onion
Salt and pepper

Method

1. Preheat a non-stick pan over a medium heat. Break the egg into a small bowl and beat lightly with a fork. Season and pour into the pan. Allow just to set, then turn over and remove from the pan. Roll it up into a cigar shape. When cool, cut it across into thin rings and reserve.
2. Thinly slice the chillies and put them in a small bowl with 1 tbsp of fish sauce and reserve.
3. In a food processor, blend the garlic, shallots and dried shrimps to a paste with 2 tbsp water.
4. Put a little of the oil in a wok and fry the chicken with the sambal olek (optional) until just done, then set aside.
5. Put more oil into the wok and fry the shrimp paste for one minute, add the bok choy, then 30 seconds later, the noodles. Keep tossing and turning to mix all the ingredients together, then add the remaining fish sauce, chicken, shrimps and chives.
6. Transfer to a large shallow serving dish and scatter the shredded lettuce over, followed by the sliced omelette. Sprinkle over the crispy red onion and serve with the bowl of sliced green chillies in the fish sauce.

Jambalaya

This recipe has been cooked and cooked by everyone I have ever taught it to and it still remains an all-time favourite. Fabulous for a crowd and if doing so simply double the ingredients.

Serves 6-8

Jambalaya:

2 heaped tbsp of creole spice plus 2 bay leaves chopped up
2 tbsp butter
100g ham, diced
100g pepperoni salami, diced
200g chicken thighs cut up, bone left in
1½ cups diced onion
2 stalks chopped celery
1 red and green pepper, cut and diced
½ cup tomato paste
2 cups of chicken stock
2 cups of uncooked long grain rice
150g frozen prawns
1 large bunch of coriander

Creole Spice (see *Essentials*)

Method

1. Heat some butter and sear chicken pieces well. Remove.
2. Heat the rest of the butter and sauté the onion, celery and peppers until softened. Add ham, pepperoni, tomato paste and 1 good tbsp of creole spice and cook together.
3. Add rice.
4. Add stock and return chicken to pan.
5. Bake covered in oven at 180°C for about 1 hour.
6. Mix in shrimps and cook for a further 15 minutes.
7. Finish off with roughly chopped coriander.

I always pan-fry in clarified butter when possible.

Just like meat, fish also benefits from time to 'relax' after it has been cooked. I always lift the fish off the heat at least 5 minutes before the end of cooking, and cover. Let it rest for 5 minutes or so. You will find your fish will be perfectly cooked every time.

Grilled Fish with Mustard and Anchovy Hollandaise and Tomato Concassé

The mustard and anchovy hollandaise is to die for.

Serves 4
4 groper steaks or any fish that has a high oil content

Quick Tomato Concassé:
Glug of oil
1 onion, chopped
5 large tomatoes, skinned and seeded
1 can organic chopped tomatoes
Salt and pepper
Chives, chopped

Mustard and Anchovy Hollandaise:
½ cup dry white wine
2 shallots, chopped
3 egg yolks
200g hot melted unsalted butter
1 tbsp seed mustard
1 tbsp anchovies, mashed

Method

Concassé

1. Heat oil, fry onion until softened, add tomatoes and canned tomatoes. Reduce until you have a thick-ish sauce. Season and add chives. I sometimes add a fresh glug of oil at the end.

Hollandaise

1. Place white wine and shallots on the heat and reduce until almost all of the wine has evaporated. Remove from heat.
2. Place the egg yolks in a blender, blend, stop, then add the wine reduction and blend together. Then slowly pour in the hot butter, adding the mustard and the anchovies at the end.

To Serve

Grill fish. Place tomato concassé on the plate, top with fish, then a dollop of hollandaise.

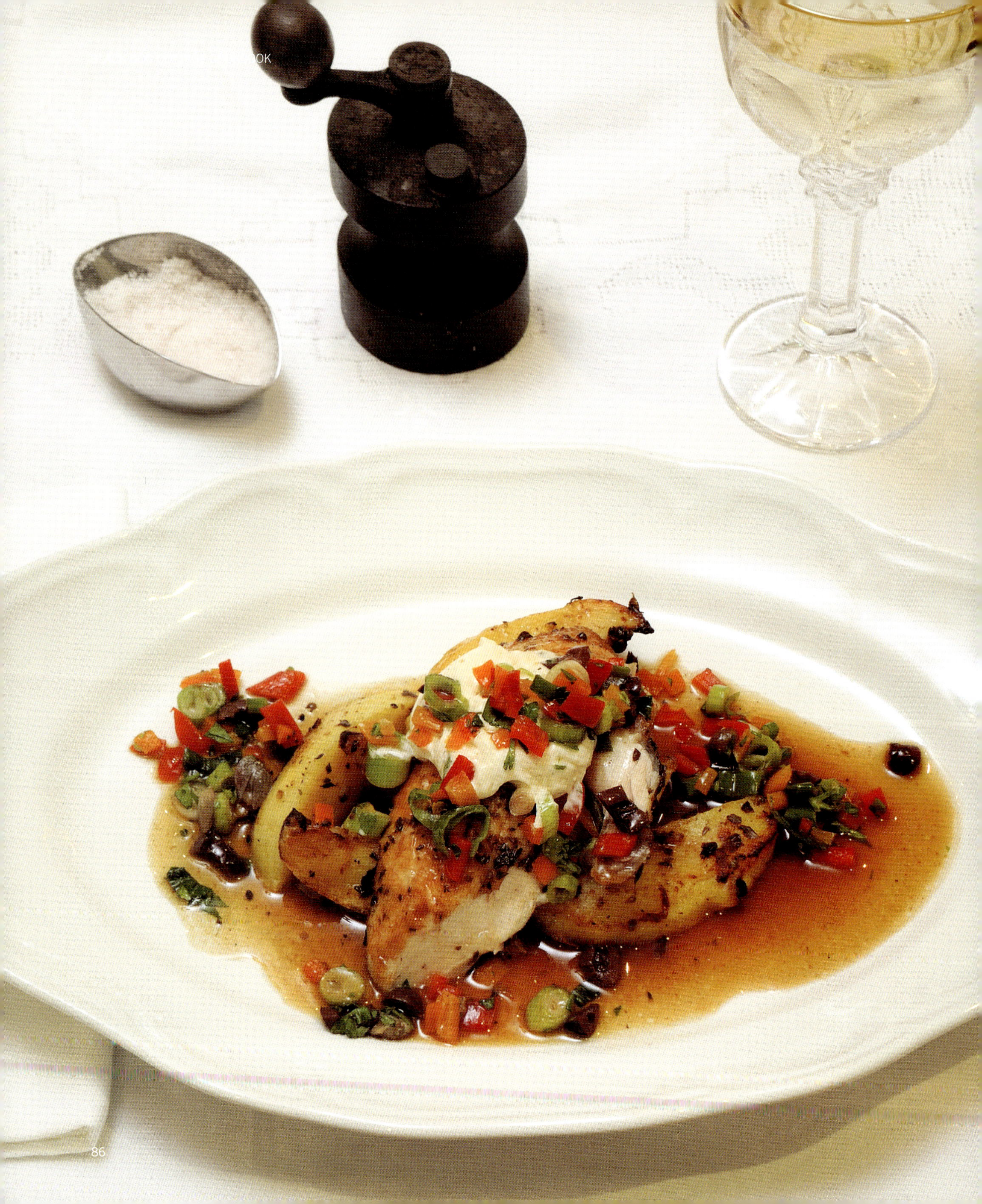

A bit of a Greek Chicken with Potatoes

This has got to be the best recipe I have ever taught. Liked universally by the old and young, without a doubt it is a hit. I like to finish it off with a dollop of aioli, lemon pickle and *jus*, or, as I have done here, with Niçoise Salad Sauce (see *Essentials* for these recipes).

Serves 4

10 garlic cloves, left whole and skin on
1 good tbsp chopped fresh thyme, oregano, or dried Greek oregano
1 organic or free-range size 14 chicken
800g potatoes, peeled
Salt and freshly ground black pepper
Juice of 1 lemon
60ml extra virgin olive oil
300ml hot water

Method

1. Preheat oven to 230°C. Throw a couple of garlic cloves and sprigs of thyme in the cavity of the bird. Tie legs together. Place chicken breast side down in a large roasting pan.
2. Slice potatoes into chips and arrange around the chicken along with the remaining garlic cloves, then pour the lemon juice over the chicken and potatoes. Season with salt and pepper, drizzle the olive oil over the top and add about three-quarters of the chopped fresh or dried thyme or oregano. Pour the hot water into the roasting pan.
3. Roast for 40 minutes, then carefully turn the chicken over. Season with a little more salt and pepper, sprinkle over the remaining fresh or dried herbs, add more hot water if needed. Reduce oven temperature to 200°C. Roast for about another 20 minutes.
4. Lift the chicken out and keep warm. Give the chips a bit more on a higher heat if need be. Serve with a lovely crisp leafy salad.

To anything green that you like to steam, add the juice of half a lemon, and a good glug of your very best olive oil. Season with salt and freshly ground pepper. Throw over some of your favourite herbs and toss.

Green Fish Curry

With green curry paste (see *Essentials*) in your fridge, this is one of those fast dinners that is easily executed at the last moment. Of course, your own home-made curry paste is far superior to any bought one. I make this curry the night before I am to serve it if possible. The flavours settle down together and it has a deeper flavour. Refrigerate overnight and bring to room temperature before reheating.

Serves 6

- 700g fish fillets (a firm variety like groper or blue nose)
- 2 tbsp ghee
- 1 tbsp green curry paste
- 2 tins coconut cream
- 1 tbsp fish sauce
- 1 tbsp lemon juice
- 2 bunches spring onions, chopped
- 2 bunches coriander, chopped
- ½ packet frozen peas

Method

1. Cut fish into nice big cubes, dry on a kitchen paper towel.
2. Heat 1 tbsp of ghee. When hot, quickly sear fish on both sides. Don't crowd the pan, but do in batches. Drain on kitchen paper towel.
3. Heat another tablespoon of ghee and fry green curry paste for 2 minutes then add coconut cream, fish sauce and lemon juice. Reduce by about one-third.
4. Add spring onions, coriander and peas. Cook for a further 5 minutes or so. Turn off and add fish.
5. Reheat gently just before you are about to serve.

My Green Fish Curry addicts

Duck Breast With Szechwan Rub

Be sure you grind the spices to a fine powder, there is nothing worse than having a mouthful of grit. If you don't have a char-grill, simply sear the duck in a very hot pan before finishing off in the oven.

Serves 4
- 30g (3 tbsp) Szechwan pepper
- 10g (1 tbsp) juniper berries
- 10g (1 tbsp) pink peppercorns
- 10g (1 tbsp) Maldon sea salt
- 1-2 tbsp redcurrant jelly
- 4 duck breasts

Method

1. Preheat oven to 200°C. Place the pepper, berries and peppercorns in the oven and dry roast for about 7 minutes. Tip them, along with the salt, into a mortar and pestle and grind until you have a fine aromatic powder.
2. Dry the duck with kitchen paper, then slit the duck skin here and there, rubbing the spices into it as well as the underside. Cover and leave for two hours or overnight.
3. Preheat oven to 220°C. Use a char-grill to sear duck (skin-side first) on both sides, then place in a hot oven for about 12 minutes. Rest covered with foil for 10 minutes. Drain off the juices that start accumulating into a jug and place in the fridge, allowing the fat to rise to the top. Underneath this fat you will have gathered a gorgeous *jus*. Reduce this *jus* in a small pan adding a good dollop of redcurrant jelly and pour over your duck to serve.

The old Woolstore, Mangakuri

Sautéed spinach is a fast and wonderful base for any dish. Pick leaves off their stems, wash thoroughly, shake off all excess water, and throw in batches into a hot pan in which you have heated a little olive oil. Turn the leaves quickly as they begin to wilt slightly, placing them on a plate. A glug of oil and a squeeze of lemon is often all that is required to add to these beautiful vibrant leaves.

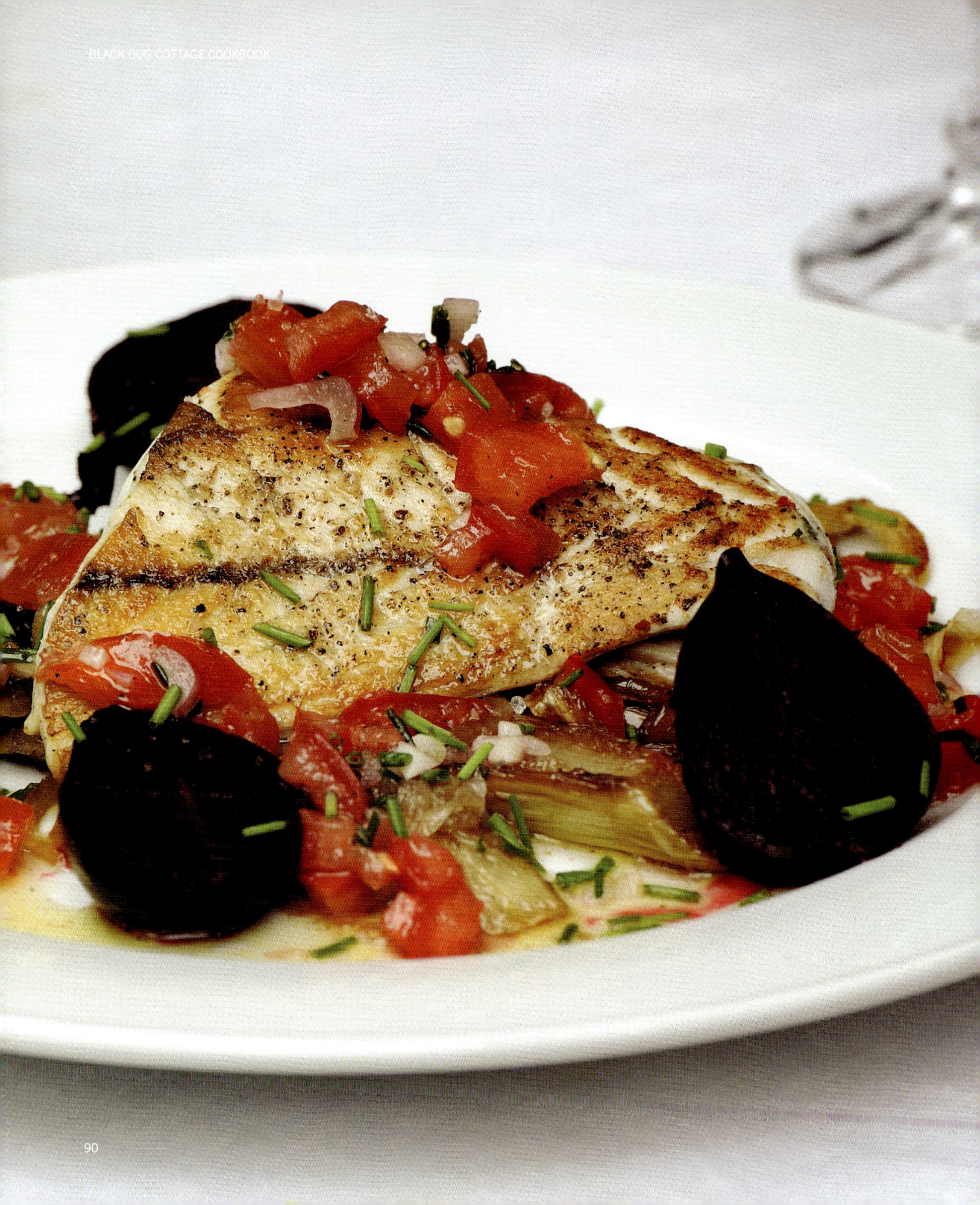

Roasted Fillet of Fish on Caramelised Onion and Fennel, Roasted Beetroot and Garlic with Warm Tomato Vinaigrette and Aioli

A very pleasing combination of all these different components. Well worth the effort and preparation.

Serves 4
4 beetroot
3 tbsp olive oil
3 brown onions, sliced finely
1 tbsp sugar
2 heads of fennel
1 head of garlic, separated
2 tsp balsamic vinegar
2 tbsp parsley, chopped
4 fillets of fish

Method
1. Wrap beetroot in tin foil and bake at 180°C for about an hour.
2. Heat 1 tablespoon of oil and sauté onions with sugar until caramelised. Set aside.
3. Heat 2 tablespoons of oil and sear sliced fennel on both sides, add garlic then finish off in a hot oven, turning over as the sides become nice and brown.
4. Combine onions, fennel and garlic together, add balsamic vinegar.
5. Heat a little oil and sear fish in a hot pan. Finish off in hot oven for about 5-7 minutes. Cooking time depends on what type of fish you have. Cover and rest for at least 5 minutes.
6. Place onion, fennel and garlic mixture in the centre of the plate. Top with fish. Place peeled and quartered beetroot around the outside along with Tomato Vinaigrette (see *Essentials*). Finish off with a good dollop of aioli and parsley.

Roasting whole spices brings out the flavour. Do this before you grind them and then keep them in an airtight jar. They do, like all spices, loose their pungency after a time.

Aegean Lamb

This sort of dish can be found all over Greece. Long, slow cooking makes it always a winner and although this recipe was somewhat inspired by Alastair Little I have changed the type and cut of meat used, along with the cooking technique, and baked it in a more Greek style. It's a great party dish and can be made ahead of time. Just be careful you don't add too much orzo, otherwise it becomes too dense. Use your eye and put in less rather than more. You can always add more orzo if you need it.

Serves 6

4 tbsp olive oil
700g onions, sliced
2 garlic cloves, sliced
2 celery sticks
2 bay leaves
2 sprigs of thyme
2 sprigs of rosemary
1 shoulder of lamb, boned, cut into large-ish cubes
900g canned tomatoes
250ml stock
500g orzo
Salt and pepper
Handful of flat-leaf parsley, chopped
Handful of mint leaves, chopped

Slow cooking equals comfort food.

It never, ever fails to excite me how the simplest ingredients can emerge from long slow cooking as something so gratifying. Tastes are transformed: melting, mellow flavours that are falling apart and utterly delicious.

Method

1. Mix the oil through the sliced onions and garlic and put half of them in a casserole dish.
2. Add a tied bouquet garni of the celery, bay leaves, thyme and rosemary.
3. Brown the lamb in a frying pan over a high heat, then arrange on top of the onions and garlic. Cover with remaining onions and garlic.
4. Pour over tomatoes and their liquid and the stock. Season well.
5. Cover with a piece of greaseproof paper and a lid.
6. Place dish in a preheated 150°C oven and bake for 1½ hours.
7. Take out of the oven and test to see if lamb is very tender. If it is not, it may require a further 20-30 minutes.
8. Remove bouquet garni and add orzo. Give it a stir around and place back in oven until pasta is cooked, about 10 minutes.
9. Garnish with parsley, mint and extra olive oil.

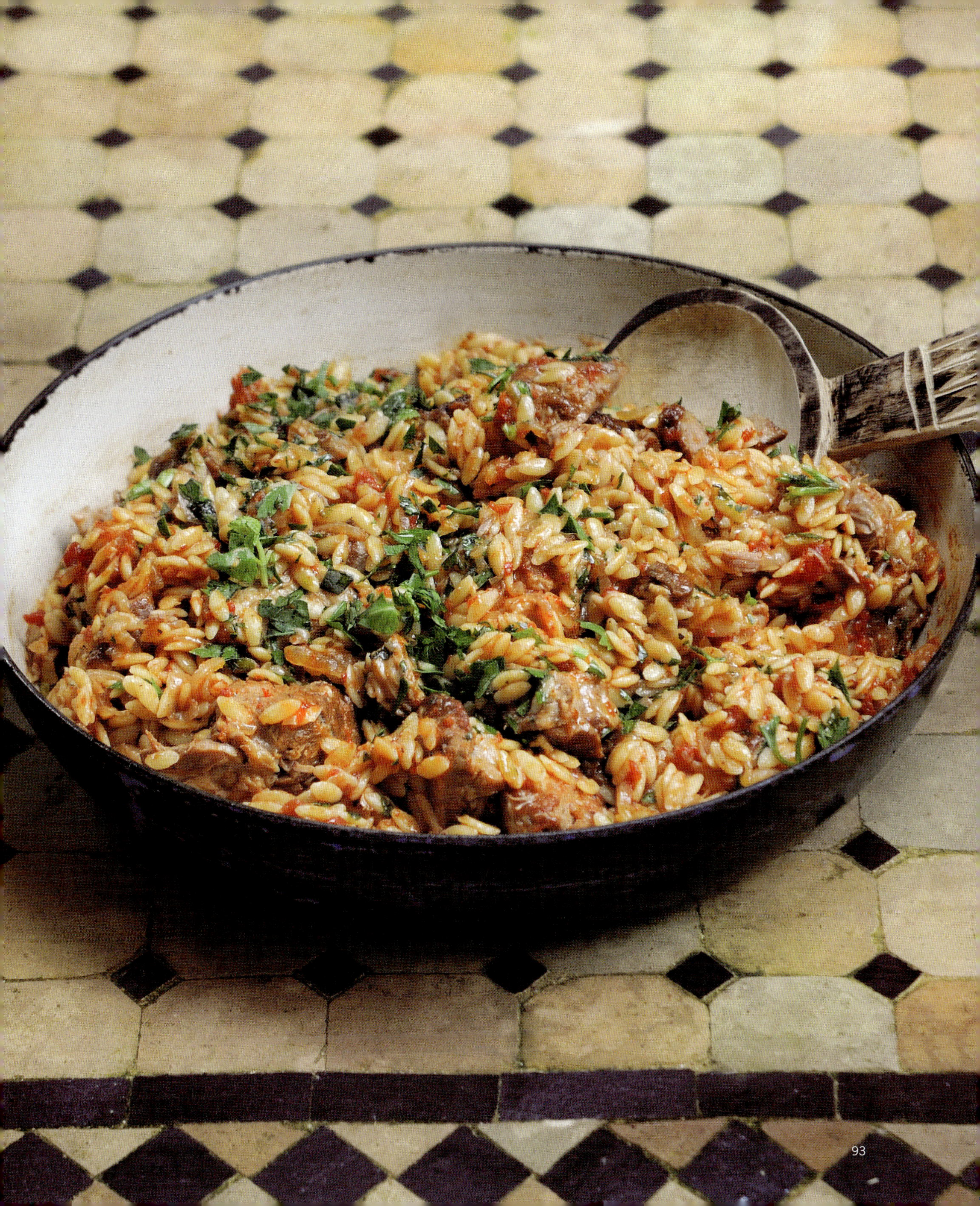

Sweetcorn, Spring Onion and Coriander Risotto with Chicken Breast, Aioli and Lemon Pickle with an Asian Sauce

Char-grill, roast or steam the chicken breast. I like to slice the breasts before I place them on top of the risotto. This makes it easier for your guests to eat. Dribble the Asian sauce around the risotto. Top chicken with aioli and lemon pickle (see *Essentials* for these recipes). It's all the different components working together in this dish that gives it a 'wow' factor.

Serves 6
6 chicken breasts

Risotto:
Approximately 1.1 litres / 2 pints of chicken stock or vegetable stock
2 tbsp olive oil
1 large onion, finely chopped
1 garlic clove, finely chopped
6 spring onions, finely chopped
440g risotto rice
Salt and freshly ground pepper
1 bunch of coriander, chopped
1 tbsp of mint, chopped
2 cobs of corn, corn removed from husk
115g freshly grated parmesan cheese

Aioli (see *Essentials*)

Asian Sauce:
2 tsp castor sugar
2 tbsp rice vinegar
1 tbsp sambal olek
Handful of coriander leaves
1 tbsp fish sauce
150ml sweet chilli sauce
Salt and pepper

Method

Risotto

1. Heat the stock. In a separate pan, heat olive oil, add garlic, onion, 3 spring onions, and corn from one of the cobs, and fry gently for a few minutes. Then add the rice. Fry the rice until it becomes slightly translucent. Then add your first ladle of hot stock, turn down the heat to a simmer, stirring all the while as the rice absorbs the stock. Add more stock as and when it has been absorbed. This will take about 20 minutes. Taste the rice, it should still have a slight bite. Remove from heat and stir in salt, pepper, coriander, mint and the left-over spring onions, corn and cheese.

Asian Sauce

1. Combine all ingredients together and let stand for at least 30 minutes.
2. While the risotto is cooking, cook your chicken breasts either by char-grilling, roasting or steaming. Remember to let them relax before slicing through and placing on top of the risotto.

The Sunday market is a great place to extend your knowledge of cooking. Just buy and try – you will be pleasantly challenged and you will learn a lot about seasonal food.

My neighbour, Vicky's vegetable garden at Mangakuri.

Pilaf of Spinach, Dill and Marinated Grilled Chicken Breast

Just like a risotto, but without all the stirring. The different layers of taste make this pilaf quite special. Enjoy it at room temperature, on its own or with anything you fancy on top, e.g. chicken (as here) or squid.

Serves 6

6 skinless boneless chicken breasts beaten lightly between plastic wrap or cling film
2 small garlic cloves, crushed
120ml olive oil
1 tsp oregano leaves, chopped
1 tsp thyme leaves, chopped
½ tsp grated lemon zest
Salt and freshly ground black pepper
300g onions, finely chopped
2 cloves garlic, crushed
125ml extra virgin olive oil
225g arborio rice
½ tsp dry roasted cumin seeds, ground
2 cups light chicken stock
1 kg spinach, washed, dried and shredded
½ small bunch of fresh dill, finely chopped
½ small bunch of flat-leaf parsley, finely chopped
Grated rind and juice of 1 lemon

Method

1. Marinate chicken breasts for 4 hours or overnight in garlic, oil, herbs, lemon, salt and pepper.
2. Sauté onion and garlic in oil until translucent.
3. Add rice and cumin, and stir for 2 minutes.
4. Pour in stock, add salt and pepper. Reduce the heat to low, cover and simmer for 10 minutes.
5. Stir in spinach, dill, parsley, lemon rind and juice. Add a little water if mixture looks dry. The pilaf should be moist. Replace lid and cook for another 10 minutes. Keep covered and set aside while grilling the chicken.
6. Wipe off marinade from chicken and grill until cooked. This will probably only take about 12-15 minutes. Keep warm giving the meat time to relax before slicing the breasts and placing on top of pilaf.

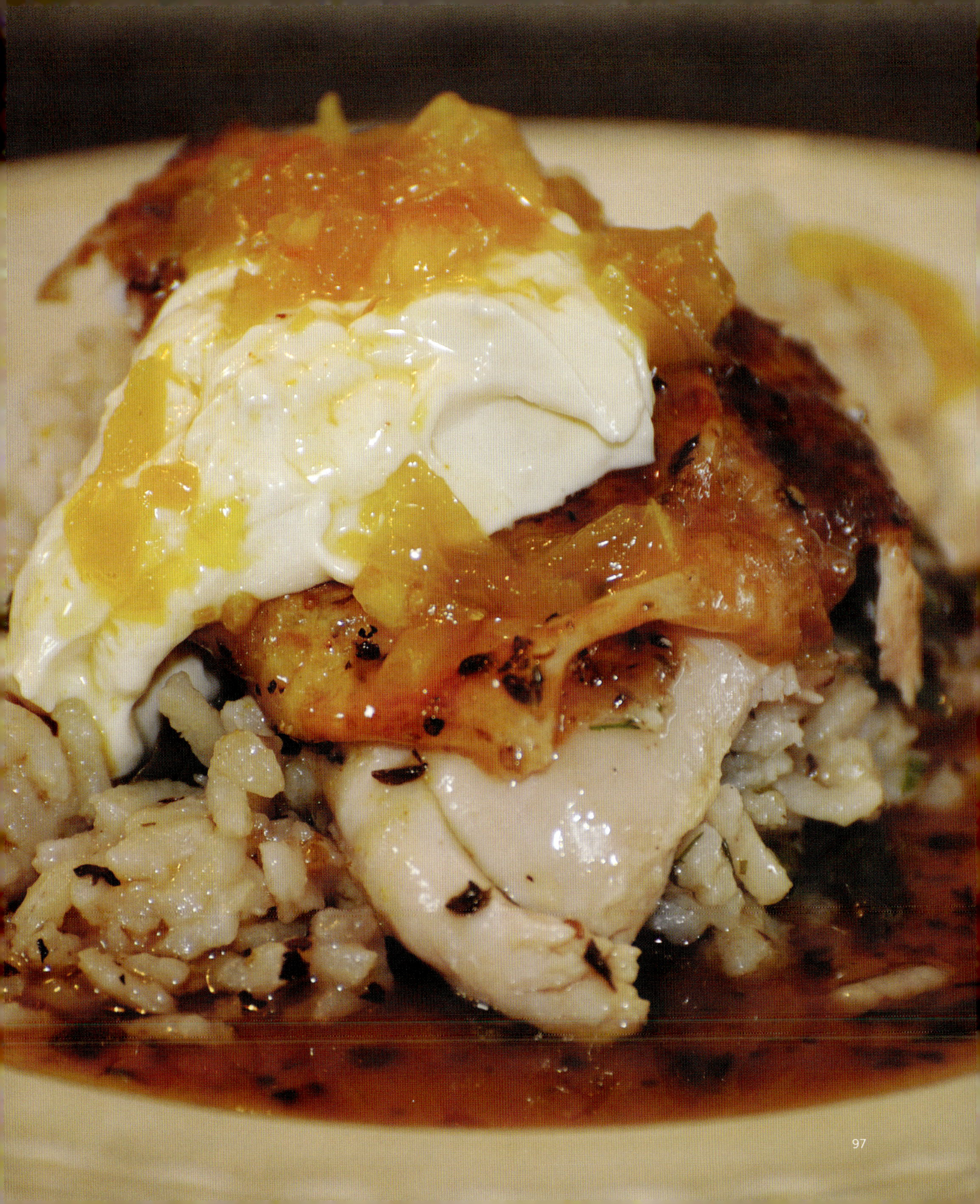

BLACK DOG COTTAGE COOKBOOK

Cooking Fish

Most fish is best cooked in one or two ways. When cooking try and keep about a half-centimetre line of pinkness running through the middle of your fish. This way when you cover and rest your fish before serving, it will emerge perfectly cooked. Here is a list of the fish that I use most frequently and how I prepare them.

Snapper
The sooner fishmongers start selling snapper with the skin on the better. Pan-fried, seared on both sides, and then finished off in a in a hot oven, or baked.

Terakihi
Pan-fried, baked in the oven with a sauce or good for a fish pie.

Tuna
Seared in a hot pan or char-grilled. Be careful that your steaks are not too thick. It is easier to keep the char-grilling short and fast, thus keeping the fish pink in the middle.

Salmon
Steamed or seared and finished off in a hot oven, baked, or poached.

John Dory
A top fish in my book, and it's enhanced by the fact that they sell it with the skin on. Pan-fry or sear and then throw into a hot oven.

Flounder
We have the best! Dust with flour that has been salt and peppered, and pan-fry.

Swordfish
Char-grill or seared and baked in a hot oven. The same applies for this fish as I have said for tuna.

Groper
Seared and finished off in a hot oven. Also good baked.

Groper Steak
Char-grilled; or steamed. Good also for baked dishes.

Gurnard
Dusted lightly with seasoned flour or egg and dipped into home-made bread crumbs. Pan-fry.

Take fresh raw salmon, skin it, cut it into bite-sized cubes, add a dab of wasabi, top with a piece of pickled ginger and toothpick it all. Place artistically on a plate along with the very best low salt soya sauce you can lay your hands on for dipping. Marvellous with drinks.

Seared Swordfish, Lemon Salsa Verde, Garlic, Potato and Rocket Mash

This is also fabulous with tuna or any other firm fish.

Serves 4

Lemon Salsa Verde

1 cup flat-leaf parsley, finely chopped
½ cup mint leaves, finely chopped
½ cup basil leaves, finely chopped
2 tbsp capers, rinsed and drained
2 cloves of garlic, crushed
⅔ cup olive oil
¼ cup lemon juice
800g potatoes, peeled and halved
⅓ cup olive oil
2 cloves of garlic, crushed
50g rocket, trimmed and coarsely chopped
4 swordfish steaks

Method

1. For the salsa, combine all the ingredients in a food processor and gradually add oil and lemon juice.
2. Cook potatoes until tender, drain, mash, and add a third of a cup olive oil and garlic. Mix well and season to taste, stir in rocket.
3. Rub a little olive oil over steaks and sear quickly on both sides in a very hot pan for about 2-3 minutes on each side.
4. Mound potato in centre of plate, top with swordfish and dribble around the sauce.

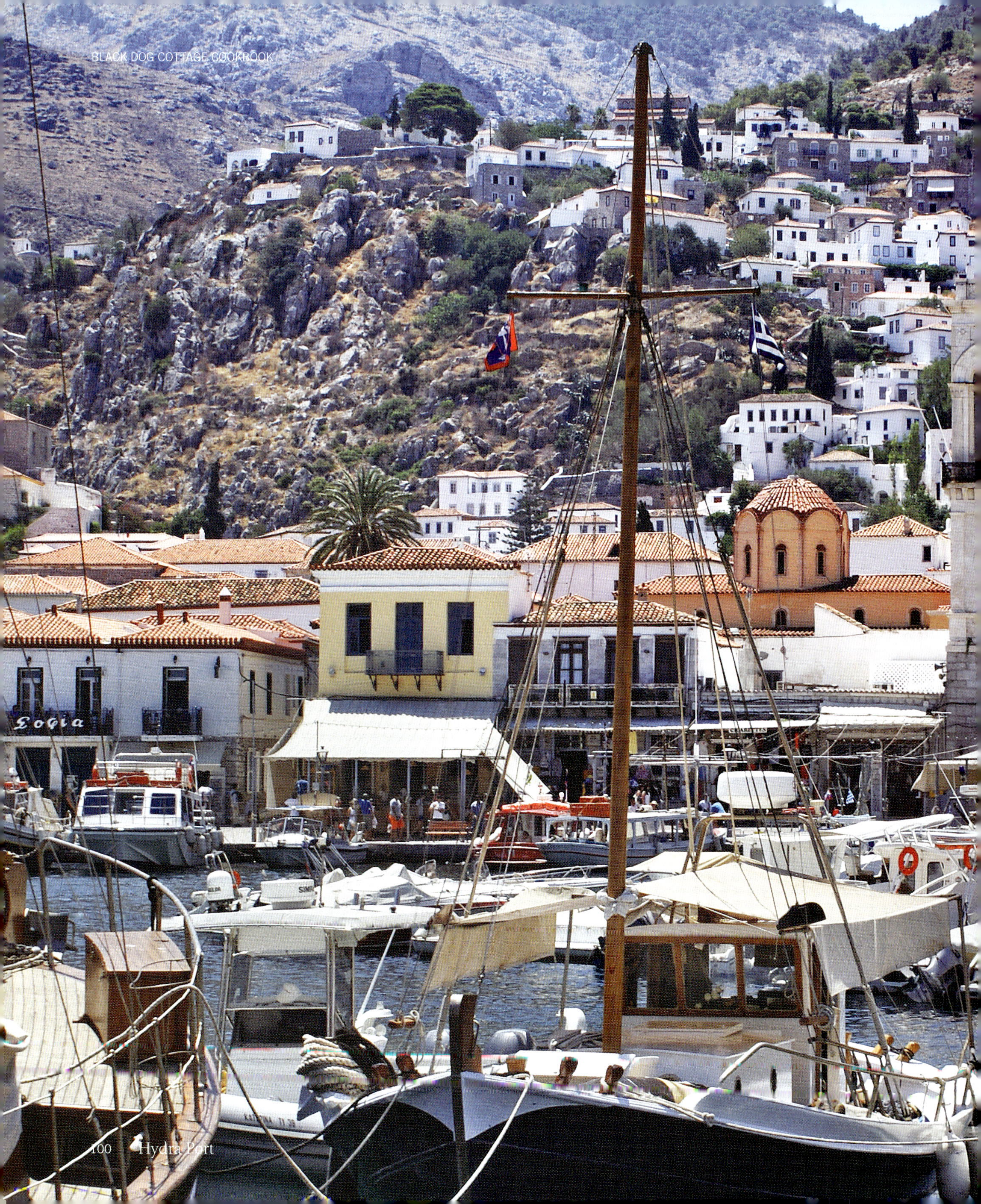

 Hydra Port

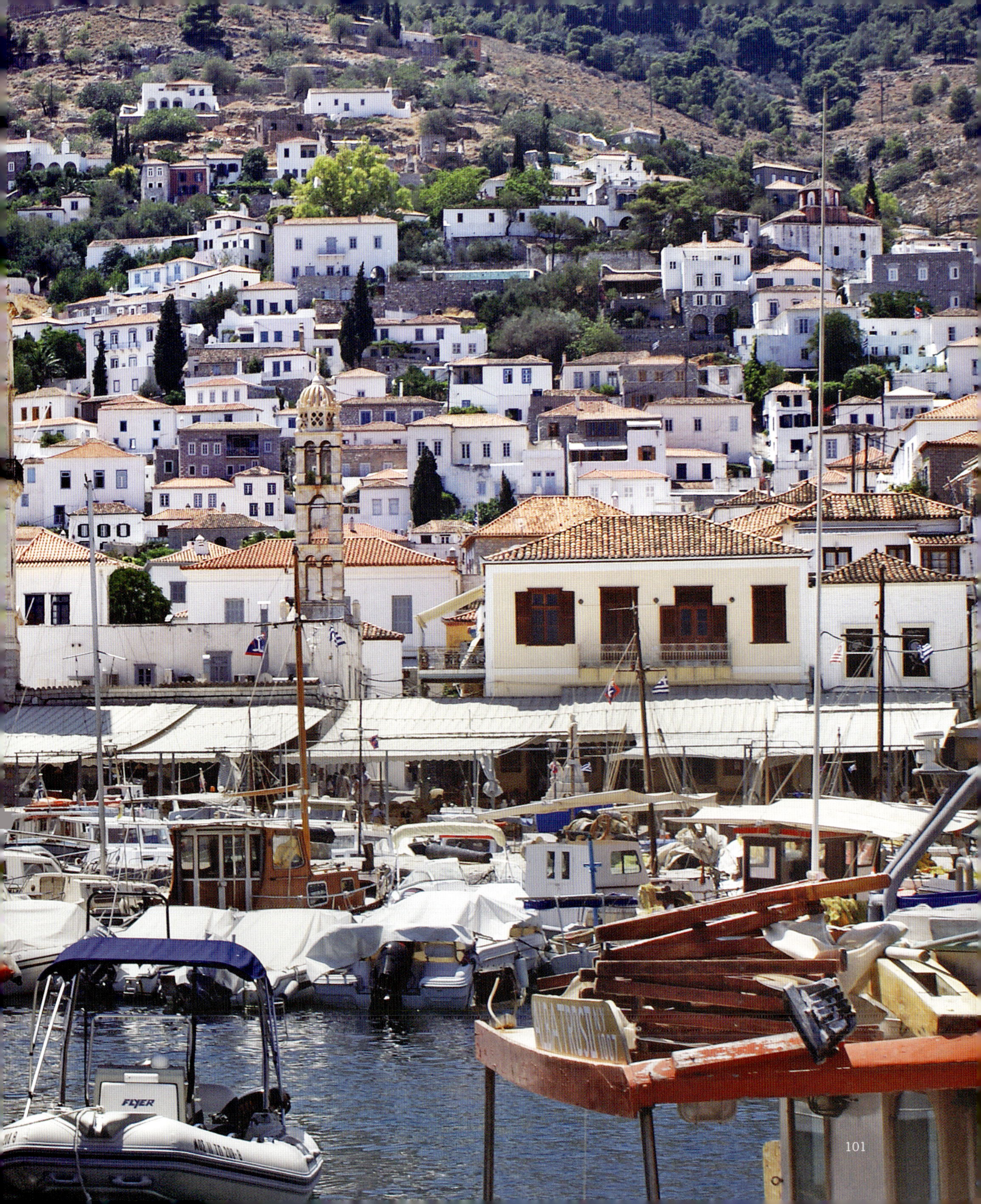
FLYER

Prawns with Tomatoes and Feta

Gorgeous and Greeky! This is one of those dishes that you want to come home and emulate straightaway. Take the time to make the fresh tomato/pepper sauce to this dish, it is well worth the trouble. I have also used a chicken breast for someone who didn't eat prawns, with great success. Serve as an entrée or as a main with a big green salad and fresh bread to drag through the remains of the delicious flavours.

Serves 4

75ml extra virgin olive oil
1 onion, chopped
1 red pepper, grilled, peeled and cubed
1kg ripe tomatoes, peeled, seeded and roughly chopped
1 tbsp sundried tomato paste
Generous pinch of sugar
Salt and freshly ground pepper
500g peeled prawns
1 tbsp chopped dill
1 tbsp chopped basil
100g feta, broken into chunks

Method

1. Preheat oven to 180°C.
2. Heat the oil in a baking dish, add the onion and sauté gently. Add the pepper, tomatoes, paste, sugar, salt and pepper.
3. Cook gently over a low heat for about 15 minutes, stirring occasionally until the sauce reduces slightly and thickens.
4. Stir in the prawns and herbs. Break up feta and place on top then bake for about 15-20 minutes or until prawns are just cooked.
5. Serve with a rocket and cos salad and lots of crusty bread to mop up the juices.

Room temperature is how I like to eat and serve all my food. I find that this way I can truly appreciate the flavours of each and every element in what I have prepared. Never eat straight from the fridge as the flavours are deadened from the cold.

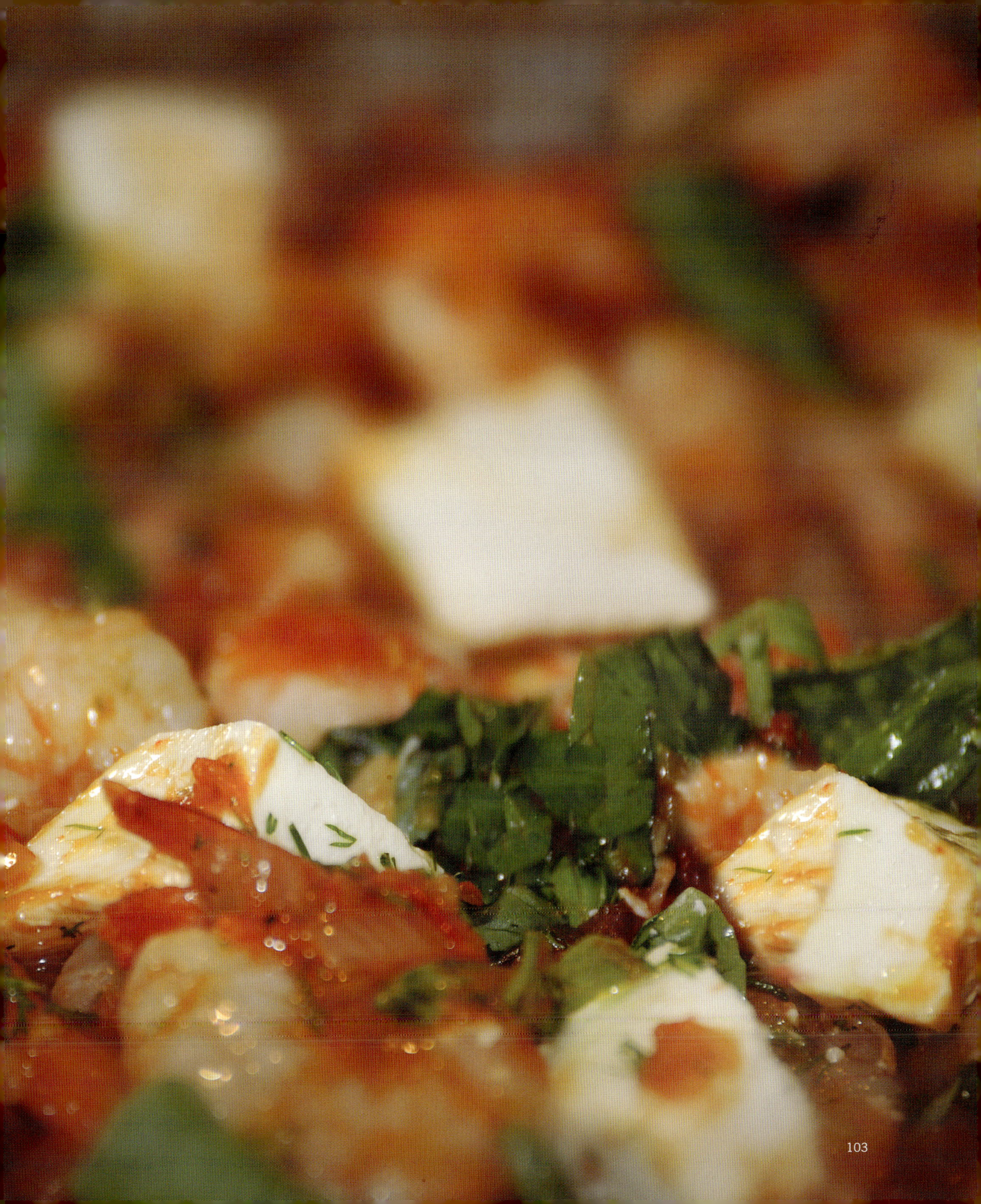

Tandoori Chicken

Great simple outdoor food. Loved by all. Serve this along side the Thai Carrot Salad (page 53), the Warm Sweet Corn Salad (page 57), Lemon pickle and Aioli (see *Essentials*) and you have the makings of a sensational meal before you. Handy hint: wear a pair of those latex gloves that you can pick up from the super market when rubbing the paste into the chicken, otherwise your fingers will smell of Tandoori all day.

Serves 4-6
¼ – ½ jar Charmaine Solomon's Tandoori Tikka Marinade
1 size 16 free-range chicken

Method

1. Totally cover chicken in marinade. Slash into the leg and thigh and rub marinade into these cuts. Tie legs loosely together. Leave overnight if possible.
2. Build a fire in your Weber and when the bricks are glowing and ready (this usually takes about 40 minutes) put in your chicken. Cook for at least 1 hour-15 minutes. Check that it is done by tipping up the chicken and watching the juices that run out – these should be clear. Cover and rest before carving.
3. Pour all the juices into a saucepan and reduce slightly for a beautiful Tandoori *jus*.

Having a giggle with Anna after a photo shoot.

We should all own a Weber barbecue. In my view, they are one of the best ways to cook large pieces or joints of meat. I find the Weber enhances meat that is left on the bone, for example, pork, lamb, turkey, and chicken. I love the way the meat comes out slightly charred and yet succulent and juicy on the inside. Because it cooks quite quickly, it is vital that you allow time for your meat to relax — even up to an hour before slicing into it.

Roasted Sirloin Strip with Watercress, Cos and Beetroot Salad

I had this at the Dank Street Depot in Sydney – it was stunning. They used scotch fillet, but I love using this cheaper cut and have made this often for picnics with great success.

Serves 6-8

3 kg beef sirloin strip
2 cloves of garlic, thinly sliced
1 stalk of rosemary, leaves only

Dressing:

100ml red wine vinegar
1 tbsp wholegrain mustard
150ml extra virgin olive oil
Salt and pepper

Salad:

1 bunch watercress, picked
1 packet of cos lettuce, chopped
4 baby beets with leaves, scrubbed and cleaned
1 avocado, chopped

To prevent avocado from discolouring wrap in paper towel before placing in fridge.

Method

1. Preheat oven to 220°C.
2. Season beef with salt and pepper. Seal all over in a hot fry pan.
3. Squash garlic and rosemary into the meat. Place beef in the oven for 15-20 minutes, for rare meat. Leave the meat to rest.
4. Drain juices from the roasting dish and reduce until almost a glaze.
5. Whisk in the red wine vinegar, mustard, olive oil, and salt and pepper.
6. Pick over watercress, taking out the tough stalks. Chop the cos into chunks. Chop the beetroot into matchsticks, place into a bowl and pour over some of the dressing. Let the beetroot marinate in this for 15-30 minutes. Add the watercress, cos and avocado to the mix. Pour over some more dressing if you need it. Serve with the beef.

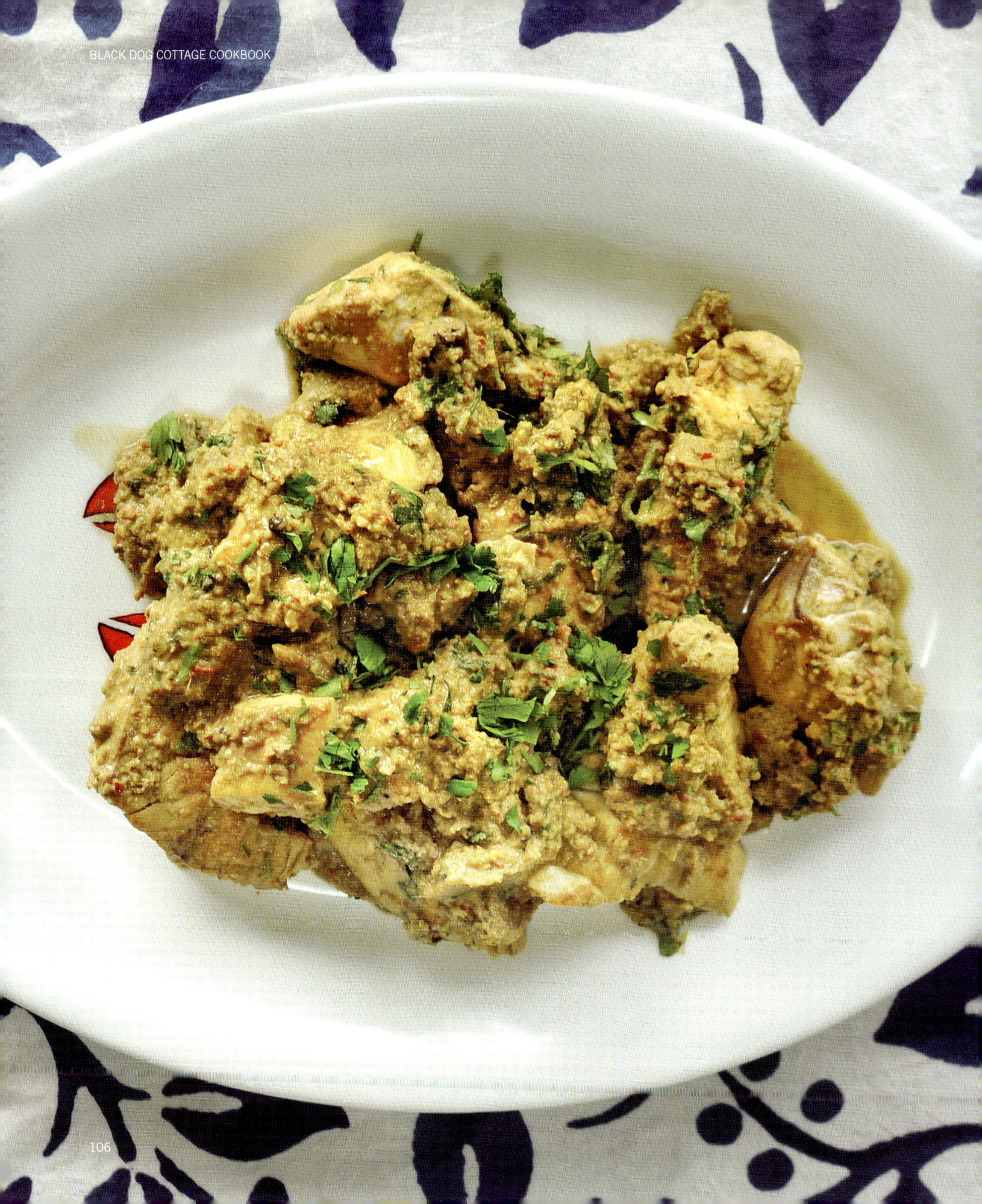

Swordfish Curry

Any firm fish will suffice, but swordfish sets this curry apart. Be sure to make this the day before serving. Time gives it a superior flavour.

Serves 6-8

2 Spanish red onions, chopped
3 fresh, long red chillies, chopped
2cm piece ginger, peeled and coarsely chopped
8 cloves garlic, halved
¼ cup vegetable oil
6 cardamon pods
8 cloves
2 cinnamon sticks
1 tsp black peppercorns
1 tbsp ground cumin
2 tsp ground coriander
½ tsp ground tumeric
400ml coconut milk
1 tsp brown sugar
1.5kg swordfish, cut into large chunks and seared
2-3 tbsp lime juice
1 bunch freshly chopped coriander

Method

1. Process onion, chilli, ginger, and garlic until paste forms.
2. Heat oil in a large pan, add paste and cook over medium heat for 5 minutes until fragrant.
3. Add dried spices and cook for a further 2 minutes, then add coconut milk, sugar and quarter of a cup of water and simmer gently for 30 minutes for flavours to develop.
4. Add fish, cover and simmer gently for 5-8 minutes, or until fish is just tender, then season to taste with salt, cracked black pepper and lime juice. Sprinkle with the coriander and serve over basmati rice.

Paella

This paella is the result of lots of reading on the subject as well as the lingering memory of the very best paella I ever have tasted in Melbourne. It is a complex and comforting dish and is a great party dish to cook and eat outdoors. If you enjoy hunting and gathering then this is a dish for you …

Serves 4-6

4 tbsp extra virgin olive oil
350g boneless chicken thighs, cut into chunks
120g chorizo (spicy if you like) cut into chunks
2 large Spanish onions, finely chopped
4 cloves garlic, chopped
1 large green pepper halved, seeded and finely chopped
250g Calasparra rice
Salt and freshly ground pepper
1 tsp smoked paprika
1 piquillo pepper, drained and sliced
1 litre chicken stock
1 tsp saffron threads
150g large prawns
Handful or so of peas
Handful of snails
Bunch of parsley, chopped
Lemon wedges to serve

Method

1. Heat a good glug of the oil in a 30-40cm paella pan or frying pan, add the chicken, brown the meat, remove and set aside. Season.
2. Add a little more oil and then fry the chorizo for a minute. Add the onion, garlic and green pepper and cook gently for about 10-15 minutes. At this stage the mixture should be starting to caramelise. Now stir in the rice, coating it with the above mixture. Return the chicken to the pan. Up to this point everything can be cooked in advance.
3. Now season with salt and pepper, add your paprika and piquillo pepper, followed by most of the hot stock, which you have flavoured with saffron threads. Let this simmer, shaking the pan from time to time. Cook for about 20-30 minutes, adding a little more stock here and there if the rice needs more cooking.
4. As you are nearing the end of cooking, evenly scatter over the prawns, peas and snails, gently pushing them down into the rice with the back of a spoon. Continue cooking until the prawns are just cooked. Scatter over with parsley. Cover with foil, turn off the heat and leave to rest for at least 10 minutes.

Wild Duck Ragout

This is an excellent way to enjoy wild duck. Of course you can successfully make it with rabbit and even venison. When using meats like venison or duck, be sure to keep the meat cubes rare. You want them to remain this way otherwise your ragout will end up tough if you overcook them. Serve with a creamy celeriac purée or potato mash and a big green salad. I always make this the night before or in the morning, allowing all the flavours to get acquainted.

Serves 6-8

Glug of oil
1 onion, finely chopped
1 carrot, finely chopped
1 celery stalk, finely chopped
2 garlic cloves, finely chopped
1 tbsp flour
2 tbsp red wine
350ml chicken stock
1 heaped dollop of tomato paste
2 large mushrooms, roasted
1 red pepper, roasted and skinned
6 duck breasts
1 tbsp Italian parsley, chopped
1 dsp thyme leaves, chopped
Salt and freshly ground pepper

Method

1. Heat oil and sauté onion, carrot, celery and garlic for about 10 minutes or just soft to the bite, then sprinkle mixture with flour and continue to cook for 3 minutes, stirring frequently, being careful not to let the flour stick and burn.
2. Add wine, stock and tomato paste. Let all this cook together adding more stock if you need it. Simmer for 8-10 minutes.
3. Cut up the mushrooms and pepper, add to the sauce. Set aside while you prepare the duck breasts.
4. Dry the duck breasts in a kitchen paper towel. Cut into good sized cubes and throw them into a very hot pan that you have glazed lightly with a little oil (do not crowd the pan, if you do this the duck will stew instead of sear). Do in batches so that the duck remains rare inside. This will probably only take a minute. Remove and put into the prepared sauce.
5. Add herbs, season with salt and pepper. Reheat carefully, making sure you don't over-cook the duck.

Ode to Doris

THE DORIS SLATER SCHOOL OF COOKING

Adie first threw open the doors of the Doris Slater School of Cooking on a warm Wellington evening in February 1992. We crowded around the rustic table in her kitchen and after admitting to being very nervous, Adie proceeded to chop and sizzle her way into our hearts. We sipped wine, watched and learned and ate to bursting point.

In that first lesson she led many of us out of the land of meat-and-three-veg into a world of exhilarating new culinary possibilities. 'Salad' then invariably meant iceberg lettuce and sliced tomatoes, coriander was relatively unknown and we hadn't branched out beyond cakes and biscuits from the Edmonds Cook Book when thanks to Adie, inspirational food suddenly became do-able and we found ourselves doing it! We found ourselves scouring Asian emporiums and obscure delis for ingredients we'd previously never heard of and to our surprise found we had it within our power to throw together food that would make people 'ooh and aah'.

Over the years Adie has continued to inspire us to be adventurous in our cooking and has earned the eternal gratitude of many of those we cook for.

Her food is exciting and imaginative and often exceptional, simply because of its simplicity. She always talks of clean unadulterated tastes. Her creed is 'fresh, fresh, fresh'. She uses only the best ingredients and avoids heavy sauces and rich concoctions that sink in your stomach. And she shrinks from food that is over-contrived or over-handled.

It is a measure of their usability that her recipes are passed from hand-to-hand, fax-to-fax, email-to-email. They pop up all over the place, often re-branded with new names such as 'Luke's Noodle Sauce' or 'Anna's Green Thai Curry Paste'. One Wellington bachelor on the dinner circuit was apparently served the same dish three times in a week following a Doris Slater course. These are recipes that work and are used time and time again.

So, thank you Adie, for giving many of us the confidence to explore food to take our everyday fare beyond the ordinary. And with my Doris folder now bursting, splitting at the seams with well-thumbed oil-splattered recipes, thank you especially for this compendium of your best.

Once again, you make things so easy.

From a Doris Devotee
February 2008

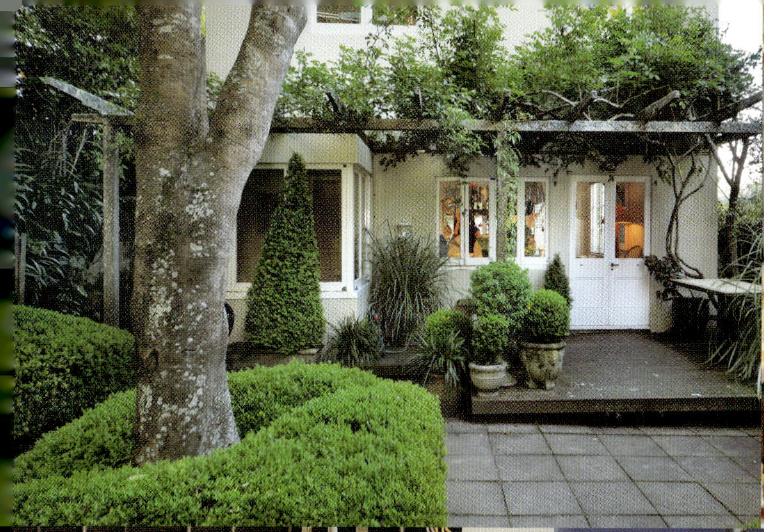

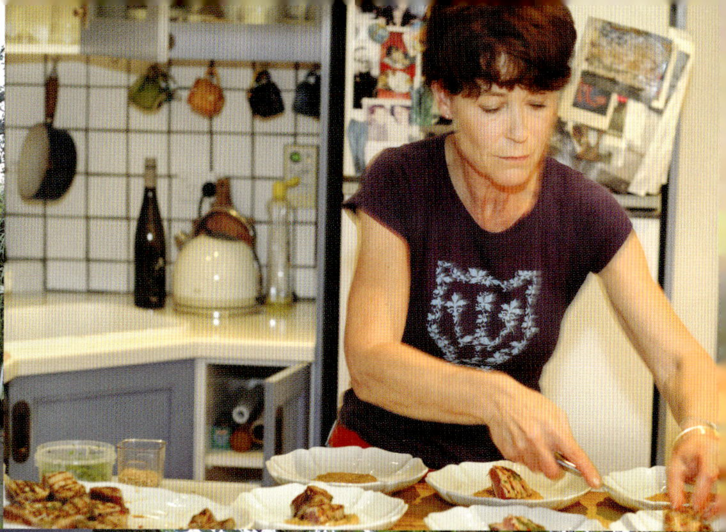

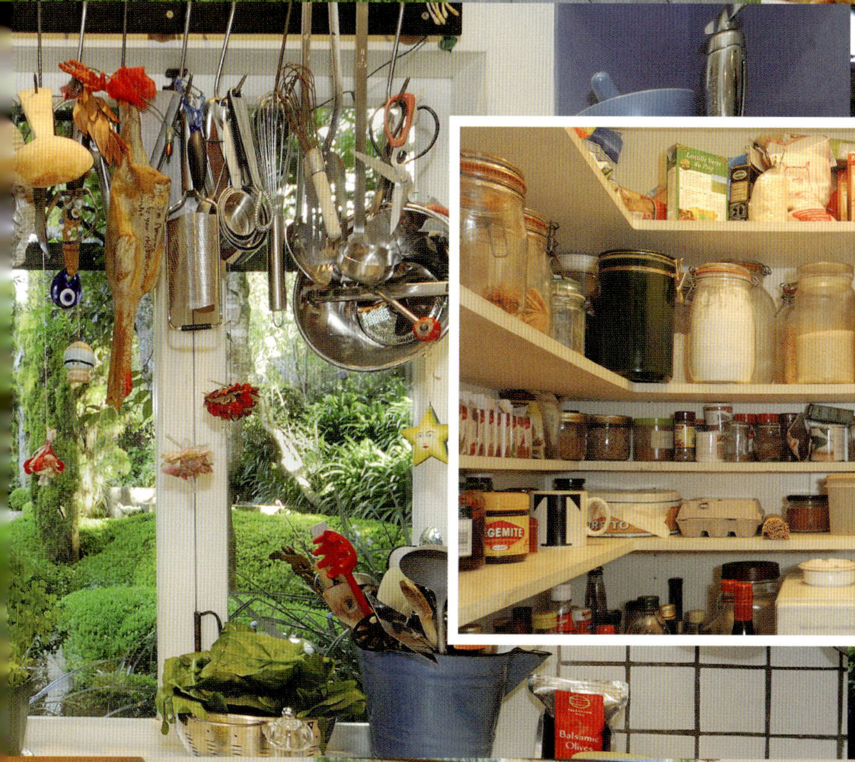
Balsamic
Olives

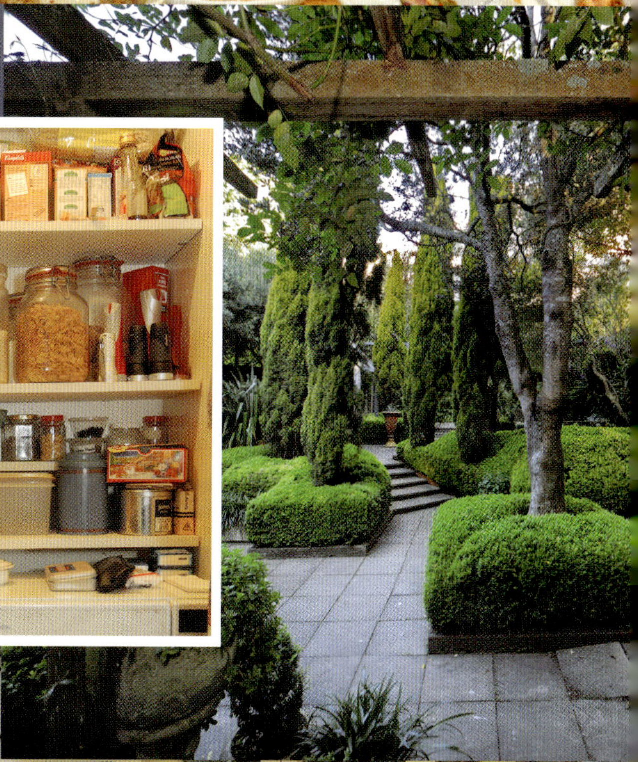

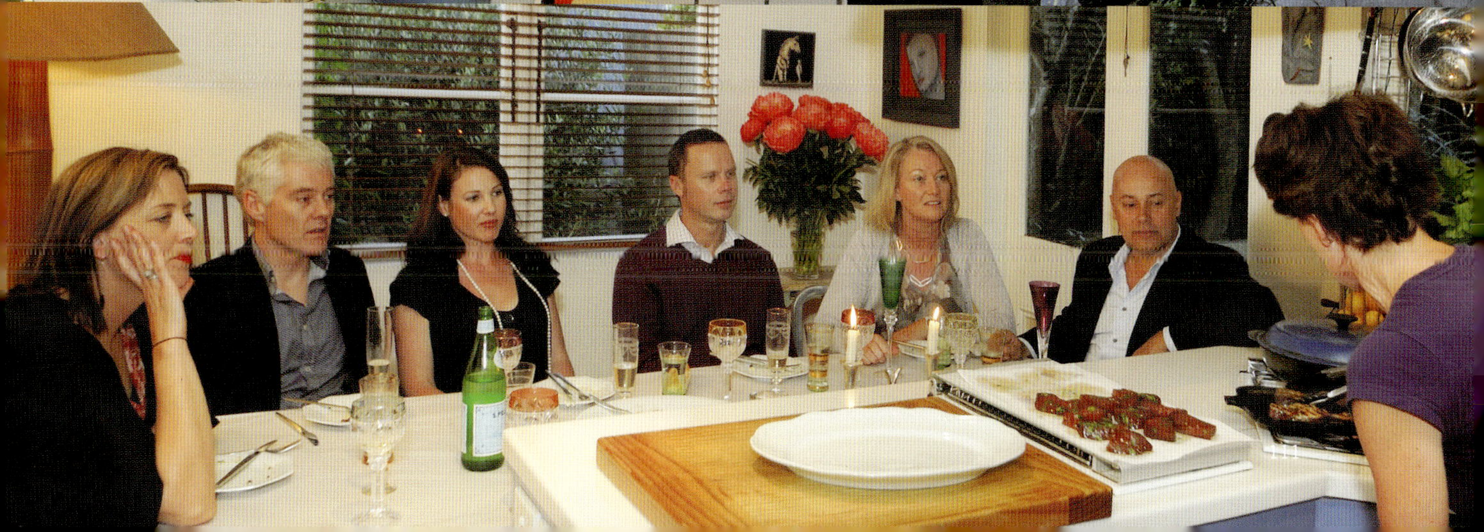

Sesame Chicken with Warm Noodles

Gorgeous summertime fare. Full of flavour and easy as you can prepare everything beforehand. I always make heaps of dressing, it keeps forever and is very delicious.

Serves 4

2 tbsp olive oil
2 garlic clove, finely chopped
6 slices fresh ginger, finely chopped
8 chicken fillets
1 aubergine, cut into slices, and then fine strips
1 carrot, cut into slices, and then fine strips
Bunch green beans, sliced thinly
400g Chinese egg noodles
200g bean sprouts
100g mangetouts, finely sliced
25g fresh coriander, roughly cut
1 tbsp sesame seeds, white and black, toasted

Dressing:

2 tbsp sherry vinegar
4 tsp balsamic vinegar
1 tsp castor sugar
100ml light soy sauce
4 tbsp sesame oil
40ml light oil
2 small chillies, seeded and finely cut
Salt and freshly ground pepper

Method

1. Mix dressing ingredients, set aside.
2. Heat half the olive oil, sauté half garlic and ginger mixture and the chicken fillets. Stir-fry for about 5 minutes or until the fillets are just cooked. Remove, keep to one side.
3. Heat remaining oil, with remaining garlic, and ginger. Add the aubergines, carrots and beans. You may have to do this in batches. Sauté until soft-ish.
4. Cook noodles, drain. Mix with bean sprouts, coriander and vegetables. Pour over the dressing, except for a few tablespoonfuls.
5. Mound noodle mixture on plates. Place chicken fillets, garlic and ginger on top.
6. Season with salt, pepper and the remaining dressing if it needs it. Sprinkle with toasted sesame seeds.

Beef Chilli with Salsa

God, I love this chilli! Fabulous meal for everyone from adults to children. Chilli always settles down overnight, so don't be alarmed if it tastes too hot to begin with and besides you've got the salsa to help cool things down, along with the addition of some sour cream which never goes astray when you're eating chilli. Cutting up the beef sets this chilli apart.

Serves 10-12

1kg chuck beef, cut into small cubes
2 tbsp medium hot chilli powder
3 tbsp olive oil
3 medium onions, chopped
8 garlic cloves, chopped
3 tbsp chilli powder
1 tbsp oregano
2 tbsp ground cumin
2 tsp salt
1 tsp pepper
3 x 400g cans of Italian chopped tomatoes
1 bottle beer
210g can tomato paste
500g red kidney beans (canned, rinsed)

For the salsa:

5 tomatoes, peeled, seeded and diced
1 cup lemon/lime juice
1 small red onion, chopped
2-3 tbsp coriander, chopped
1 garlic clove, chopped

Our local butcher on Hydra

Method

1. Combine beef cubes and chilli powder together. Leave to marinade overnight.
2. Heat a little oil in pan and sear beef in batches; transfer to a large skillet.
3. Heat the balance of the oil and add the onions, cook for 5 minutes then add garlic, chilli, oregano and cumin, salt and pepper. Stir for 3 minutes, then transfer to skillet.
4. Stir in tomatoes, beer and tomato paste, bring to the boil, reduce heat and simmer until tender. This could take up to about 3 hours. I sometimes do this in an oven on about 140°C
5. Add beans and leave overnight if possible, for flavours to get acquainted.
6. Combine all ingredients for the salsa. Serve with rice and a dollop of sour cream.

Spaghetti with Aubergine, Chilli and Tomato

When aubergines are in season, be sure to make this simple sauce. You can also use it as a base for any dish or chopped up a little and put on crostini for drinks.

Serves 4

450g aubergine
1½ tbsp extra virgin olive oil
2 red onions, sliced
1½ tsp garlic, chopped
400g tomatoes, peeled, seeded and diced
1 tbsp dried tomato paste
1 red chilli, chopped
3 tbsp parsley, chopped
450g spaghetti
Pepper to taste
Shaved parmesan

Method

1. Slice aubergine. Sprinkle with salt for 30 minutes. Rinse and pat dry.
2. Brush aubergine slices well with oil and dry roast, char-grill or pan-fry them until they become brownish on both sides.
3. Sauté onions and garlic until soft in oil, then add tomatoes, tomato paste, and chilli. Cook until you have a good consistency for a sauce. Now add parsley and sliced aubergines that have been cut into slivers about 1cm wide.
4. Serve sauce on top of cooked spaghetti. Shave parmesan over and serve.

modern GREEK
the real greek at home
DISHES FROM THE HEART OF THE GREEK KITCHEN

rena salaman
simple seasonal
A FRESH LOOK AT MEDITERRANEAN

Fab Chook Pie

A favourite. I make it all year round and it never fails to receive rave reviews.

Serves 6

1 size 14 organic chicken
1 tbsp extra virgin oil
1 leek, white part only, finely sliced
1 onion, finely chopped
1 garlic clove, chopped
1 bunch spring onions, finely chopped
1 tbsp flour
300ml chicken stock
2-3 courgettes, thinly sliced and steamed
1 cup frozen peas
1 tbsp chives, snipped
1 tbsp Italian parsley, chopped
1 dsp tarragon or chervil, chopped
Salt and pepper
1 pkt puff pastry
1 egg, beaten with a splash of water for glazing

Method

1. Loosely tie the chicken legs together and steam chook for about 45 minutes. Turn off and let chicken cool down in steamer until cool enough to handle. Take out, skin and chop chicken into good size pieces, collecting all the juices that fall from the chicken as you go. Set aside.
2. Heat oil in a large flat pan. Sauté leek, onion and garlic until soft. Add spring onions, continue to sauté for another few minutes.
3. Sprinkle with flour and cook the flour with the sautéed vegetables for 4 minutes or so, then add your stock and the juices that you have saved from the chicken. You can add a splash of white wine here if you wish. Cook together for 10 minutes, you may need to add extra stock or water but what you want is quite a thick sauce so that when you slice the pie the inside isn't too runny and it doesn't spill out everywhere.
4. Add the courgettes, peas, chives, parsley, tarragon, salt and freshly ground pepper and chicken. Combine well and cool mixture down a little.
5. Heat your oven to 200°C.
6. Lay the pastry out on a tray and brush with beaten egg around the sides. Cut a second sheet of pastry into four and stick each piece onto each side of the pastry to make a larger base. Pile the chicken pie mixture onto pie base and make a larger top as you have done with the bottom to cover. Seal sides together, cut a slit in the top of the pie to let the steam escape, and glaze the pie.
7. Place pie in pre-heated oven and bake for about 20 minutes or until pastry is golden and cooked through.

Baked Snapper with Vegetables

This tastes of Greece. It can be made in advance and gently reheated, just be sure you don't overcook the fish. It's delicious eaten at room temperature. I have also made this with terakihi with great success.

Serves 6

6 large snapper fillets
Juice of one lemon
2 tbsp olive oil
½ tsp salt
10 tomatoes peeled, seeded and chopped
1 onion, finely chopped
2 stalks of celery, finely chopped
1 tsp chopped fresh rosemary
60ml extra virgin olive oil
1 heaped tbsp dried tomato paste
225ml white wine
1 bunch of baby carrots, lightly steamed
3 courgettes, sliced into rounds, lightly steamed
2 large waxy potatoes, sliced and steamed

Method

1. Place the snapper fillets in a large bowl. Combine the lemon juice, olive oil, salt, tomatoes, onion, celery and rosemary in another bowl. Pour over the fish, cover and refrigerate for 1-2 hours.
2. Preheat the oven to 220°C. Remove the snapper fillets from the marinade. Set aside.
3. Pour the marinade into a saucepan. Add the extra virgin olive oil and cook over a moderate heat for 5 minutes. Add the dried tomato paste, the wine and simmer for another 15 minutes. Set aside to cool.
4. Place the fillets in a large flat dish. Toss all the vegetables together. Use this mixture to cover the snapper fillets. Pour the wine sauce over the top. Bake in the oven for 20-30 minutes or until the snapper is just cooked.
5. Serve with lots of crusty bread.

Always remember that we learn and grow through our mistakes, and so it is with cooking. Embrace a mistake and see it as a challenge to improve and change.

Preserved Lemon Marinated Leg of Lamb

Cook this lamb in a Weber if you have one if not, bone out the leg of lamb and barbecue it, using the grill and hot plate. I don't like my lamb to be too pink and giving cooking times is fraught with variables. So I urge you to trust your instincts to choose the right cooking time for your desired result. The resting marinade is essential to the taste of the lamb and combines deliciously with the meat juices.

Serves 6

2kg leg of lamb
2 garlic cloves, sliced
2 anchovies, chopped
1 tbsp coarsely grated lemon rind
2 sprigs fresh rosemary, leaves picked and roughly chopped
60ml (¼ cup) extra virgin olive oil
Generous glug of verjuice
3 bay leaves

For the resting marinade:

2 preserved lemon quarters or 2 dollops of lemon pickle
80ml (⅓ cup) extra virgin olive oil
60ml (¼ cup) verjuice
3 shallots or spring onions, finely sliced
⅓ cup freshly chopped flat leaf parsley

Method

1. Combine the garlic, anchovy, lemon rind and rosemary sprigs all into a food processor and, using the pulse action, add the oil until you have a rough paste.
2. Make incisions in the fat of the lamb and insert paste. Smear any left-over paste over the lamb. Sprinkle lamb with verjuice and dot with the bay leaves. Refrigerate for several hours to marinate.
3. Prepare your Weber. When ready, cook the lamb as you normally would. For me, this is about 1 hour 40 minutes.
4. To make the resting marinade, discard pulp from lemons and dice flesh, then combine with remaining ingredients. Pour marinade into a baking dish large enough to hold the lamb. When lamb is done to your liking, slip lamb into resting marinade. Rest for 20 minutes, turning once or twice.
5. Serve sliced with marinade and jus.

Hydra, sunset

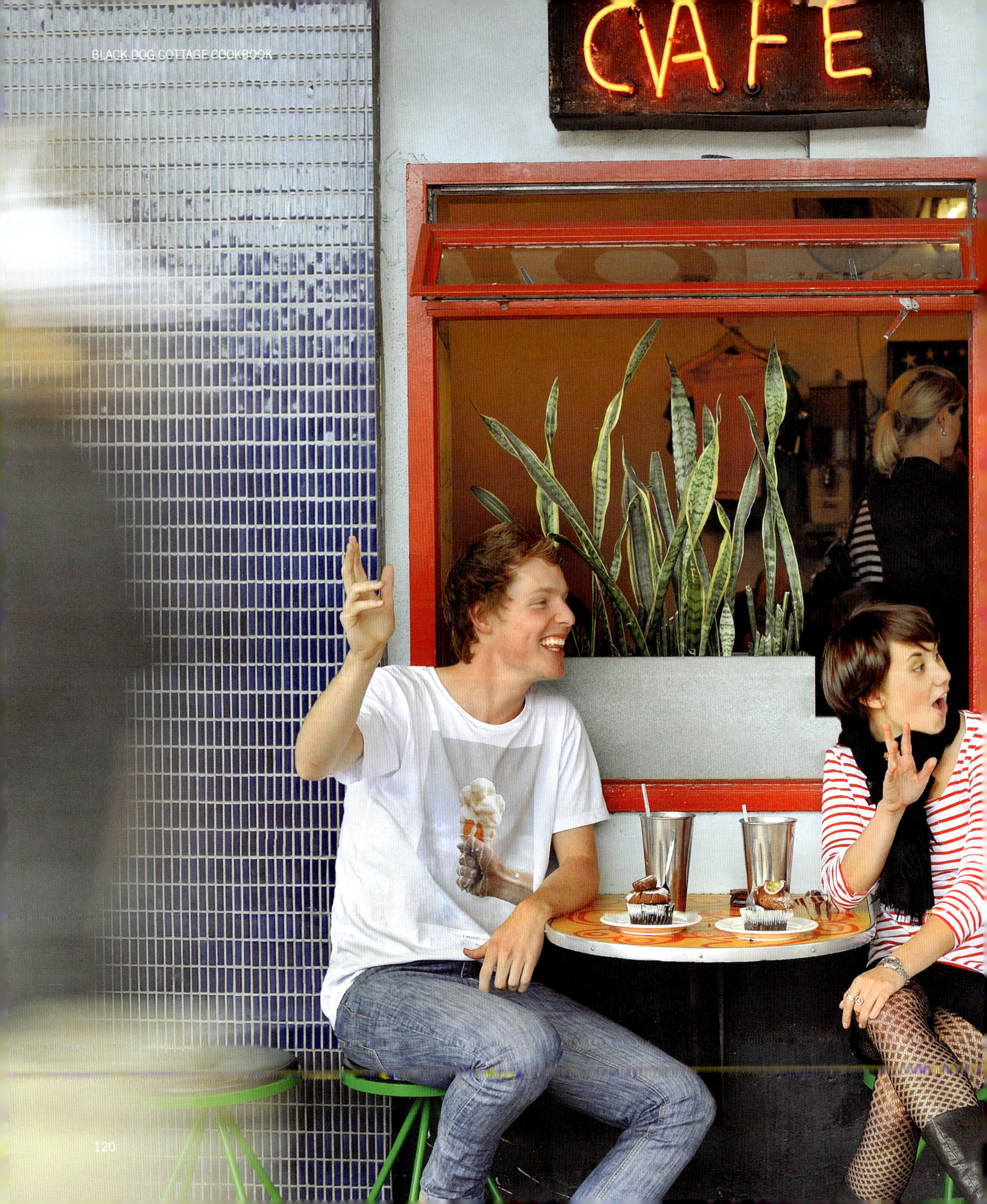
CAFE

Sweet Things

These are a few of my favourite puddings and cakes. I tend to make them frequently because they are quick and easy and everybody loves them, no matter how often you serve them.

Just like the rest of your meal, the weather and season can help to shape your choice of pudding. Some puddings such as Downtown Chocolate Mousse or Glazed Lemon and Mascarpone Tart can be served any time of the year. Never underestimate a simple fruit salad, it is often the perfect end to a meal. Whatever you choose, your dessert should be uncomplicated, making use of what's to hand.

Rules for Making Cakes

Here are a few simple rules for making cakes:

1. Make sure the butter is soft before you start.
2. Cream the butter and sugar really, really well before adding any other ingredients.
3. Sift the dry ingredients from a good height to add a lot of air.
4. Add the dry ingredients to the wet ones in stages, folding them in (never beating) as lightly as possible.
5. Always use a springform tin – which you have buttered, floured and lined with baking paper.

Mascarpone and Raspberry Crème Brûlee

A sensational dessert. The raspberries cut through the dense richness of this pudding, adding just the right edge.

Serves 8

225g raspberries
8 egg yolks
50g castor sugar
100g mascarpone
500ml whipping cream
Demerara sugar

Method

1. Divide raspberries between 8 ramekins.
2. Whisk together yolks, castor sugar and mascarpone.
3. Bring cream to the boil, then pour onto the egg yolk mixture and blend well.
4. Return mixture to a gentle heat, stirring constantly until it thickens (about 30 minutes).
5. Divide mixture between ramekins and chill overnight.
6. Sprinkle demerara sugar over the tops of the ramekins and place under a hot grill, to melt and caramelise the sugar, or if you have a blow torch do it with this. Chill again for an hour or so before serving.

Summer Cake with Raspberry and Almond

A stunning and beautiful cake. Delicious served warm with lightly whipped cream. Try it with any fruit that's in season.

Serves 8

2 cups icing sugar
⅔ cup self-raising flour
2 cups ground almonds
2 tbsp orange zest
8 egg whites
185g butter, melted
1½ tbsp whole milk
200g raspberries
Castor sugar to sprinkle on top

Method

1. Preheat the oven to 180°C.
2. Butter, flour and line a 24cm cake tin with baking paper.
3. Sift together the icing sugar and flour into a large bowl and stir in the ground almonds and orange zest.
4. Lightly mix egg whites in a bowl to break them down. Add them, along with the melted butter and milk, to the sugar and flour mixture.
5. Fold through half the raspberries and pour the mixture in the prepared tin. Fold lightly; it is important that you do not over-mix.
6. Scatter over the rest of the raspberries and castor sugar. Bake for about 1 hour 15 minutes, until a skewer comes out clean. Allow to cool slightly before removing from the tin.

Always use organic free-range eggs –
their flavour is vastly different from any other egg on the shelf.

Grilled Pineapple

The pineapple caramelises and is utterly delicious. Serve with lashings of lightly whipped cream, some softly whipped goat's curd or yoghurt.

Serves 6
1 large pineapple
4 tbsp honey
75g butter

Method
1. Peel the pineapple and cut into wedges 1 inch thick. Melt the butter, stir in the honey and pour over the pineapple. Marinate for at least 1 hour.
2. Remove the pineapple from the marinade, reserving the marinade. Place pineapple on an oiled grill over a medium low heat. Cook until golden, turning and brushing with the reserved marinade.

Summer Pudding

This is very impressive as well as being utterly divine. Excellent for a special occasion like Christmas.

Serves 8

8 large thin slices of white bread (crusts removed)
100ml water
9 leaves gelatine
250g strawberries
250g raspberries
250g blackberries
Enough sugar to sweeten berries, depending on season
Extra raspberries for sauce

Method

1. Line a mould with slices of bread.
2. Soften the gelatine in water.
3. Divide gelatine liquid between 3 saucepans.
4. Put the strawberries in one pan, the raspberries and blackberries in the other two. Stew gently, adding enough sugar to sweeten.
5. Make alternate layers of fruit and bread in mould. Finish with a layer of bread.
6. Make a hole in the centre and pour in any remaining fruit juice.
7. Cover the top with a round piece of baking paper, (so that your weight does not stick to the bread) place a saucer over that and weigh down with something heavy. Allow to set in the refrigerator overnight.
8. Make a sauce by blending extra raspberries and enough castor sugar to sweeten in the blender.
9. When pudding has set, turn out onto a dish and pour over sauce. Decorate with fruit and sprinkle with icing sugar.

Leaf gelatine is far preferable to powdered. It sets food in a softer and much more natural way. Soak the leaves in cold water for a few minutes, or until they become soft, then squeeze out moisture before adding to the warm mixture in which they will dissolve.

Sticky Date Pudding

Always a winner. Serve in the depths of winter by the fire, with lashings of cream. A dessert that travels well, it's always appreciated if you turn up with this in hand.

Serves 8-10

185g stoned dates
250ml water
1 level tsp baking soda
60g butter
2 eggs
185g sugar
185g self-raising flour
¼ tsp vanilla essence

Sauce:

150g brown sugar
150ml cream
½ cup butter
½ tsp vanilla essence

Method

1. Cook dates in water until they reach a jam-like consistency.
2. Beat in remaining ingredients and mix well.
3. Butter and flour a jam roll tin, pour in mixture. Bake at 190°C for 25 minutes.
4. Place all sauce ingredients in a pan, bring to the boil and boil for 5 minutes.
5. Serve pudding and sauce together with whipped cream.

Castle Rock, Mangakawi

Hand-whipped cream is far superior to any other. Be sure that you pour your cream into a large clean bowl and have a good-sized balloon whisk. I often hand it to my guests to do. I don't think they mind, in fact I think they quite like it! The cream holds its form better, it does not separate and the texture is completely different – softer and fuller.

Semifreddo Nougat Ice Cream

Perfect ending to any meal, although not for the faint-hearted but I think you'll find even they will be persuaded to try this. The nougat is an expensive addition. You can, of course, add anything you like, but I love the contrast of all that softness surrounding the crunch of the nougat!

Serves 8

8 egg yolks
220g (1 cup) castor sugar
400ml pure cream
400g mascarpone
1 tsp vanilla extract
300g brittle nougat, coarsely chopped

Method

1. Place the egg yolks in the bowl of an electric mixer and whisk until pale and combined.
2. Gradually add the castor sugar and whisk until light and creamy.
3. Add the cream, mascarpone and vanilla and whisk until thick-ish.
4. Add the nougat and fold through the ice-cream mixture until well combined.
5. Pour into a container and freeze overnight.

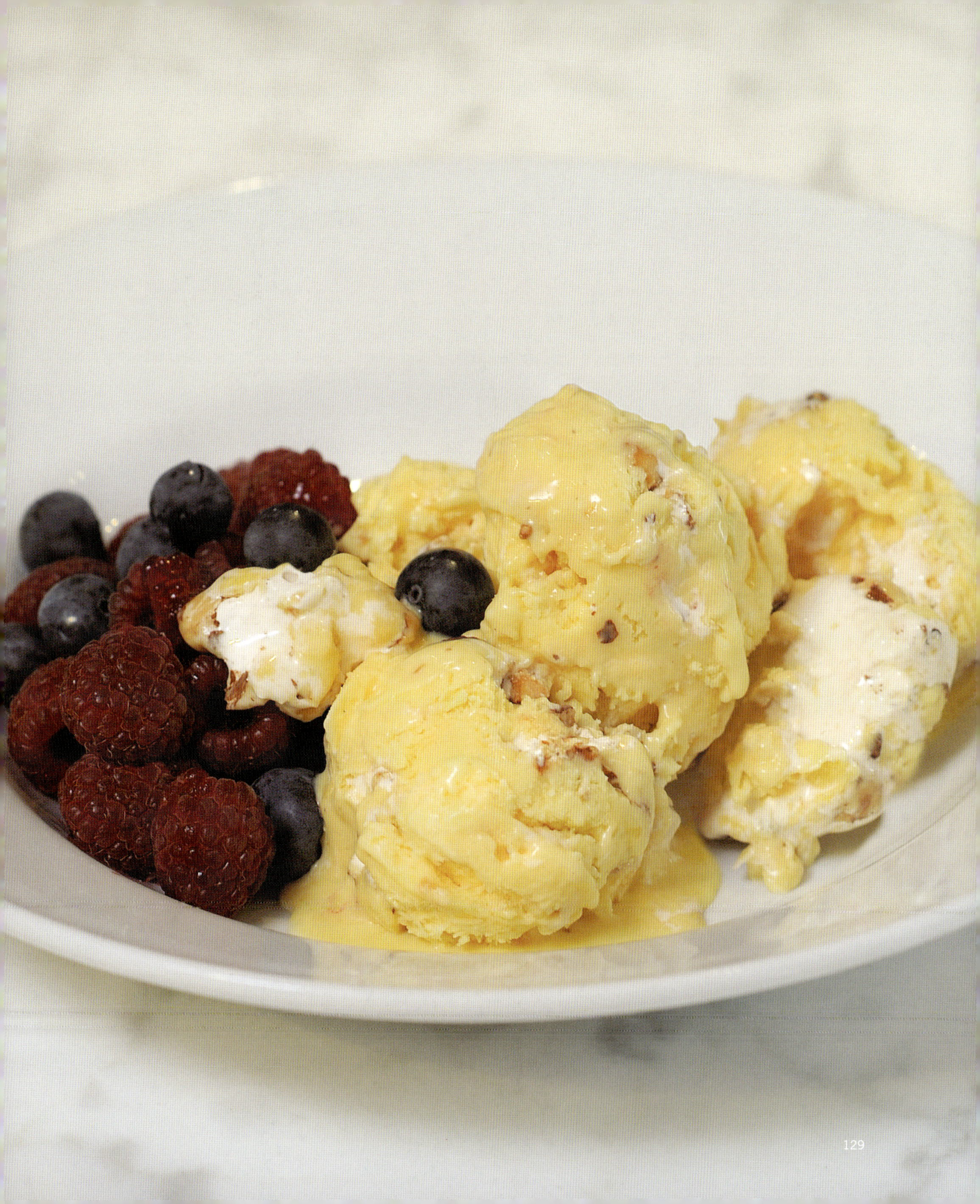

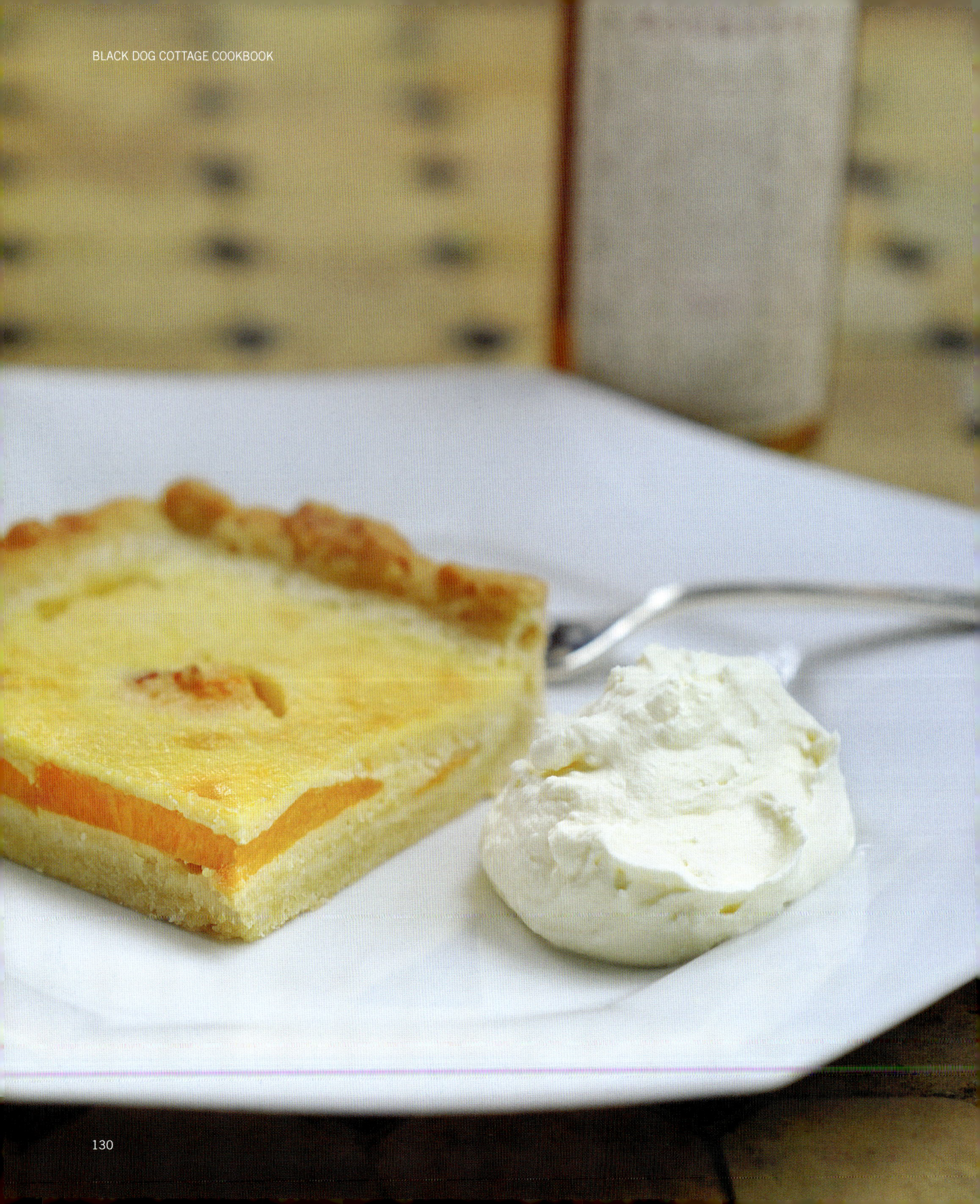

Peach Clafoutis

Make this dessert with any fruit that's in season. The pastry can be rather fragile so I usually roll it out between two pieces of baking paper or sometimes I just end up pushing the pastry into the tart tin with my fingers that have been dipped into flour.

Serves 8

Pâté Sableé (see below)
4 medium peaches
4 tbsp whipping cream
2 whole eggs
20g butter
3 tsp vanilla sugar
3 tbsp ground almonds
1 tbsp kirsch

Method

1. Pre-heat oven to 200°C.
2. Roll out pastry, place in a 25cm tart tin and prick the sides and bottom of pastry with a fork. Chill in refrigerator for 10-20 minutes. Blind bake for 15 minutes.
3. Peel and slice fruit.
4. Put eggs, cream, vanilla sugar, ground almonds and kirsch into large bowl and mix together thoroughly with a whisk.
5. Melt butter and pour into batter. Whisk well.
6. Spread fruit over tart base and pour over batter.
7. Cook for 25 minutes.

Pâté Sableé – Sweet Flan Pastry:

500g plain flour
100g ground almonds
Grated rind of a lemon
150g castor sugar
Pinch salt
380g butter
1 whole egg
2 egg yolks
3 generous tbsp dark rum

Method

1. In a food processor, proceed as follows:
2. Place the flour, ground almonds, grated lemon rind, sugar and a pinch of salt into the food processor. Cut the butter into cubes and add, together with the whole egg, egg yolks and rum.
3. Put the machine on top speed. Stop as soon as you have a homogenous paste, do not overwork. Collect up the pastry, wrap in plastic wrap and refrigerate until needed.

Roasted Nectarines with Berries and Mascarpone

Serves 6

9 nectarines
50g soft brown sugar
250g raspberries
Mascarpone
25g flaked almonds

Method

1. Preheat oven to 150°C.
2. Cut nectarines in half, remove stones. Place on baking tray, sprinkle with sugar and roast for about 1½ hours.
3. Remove from oven and let them cool down. Serve 3 halves per person with fresh berries and mascarpone. Scatter over some flaked almonds.

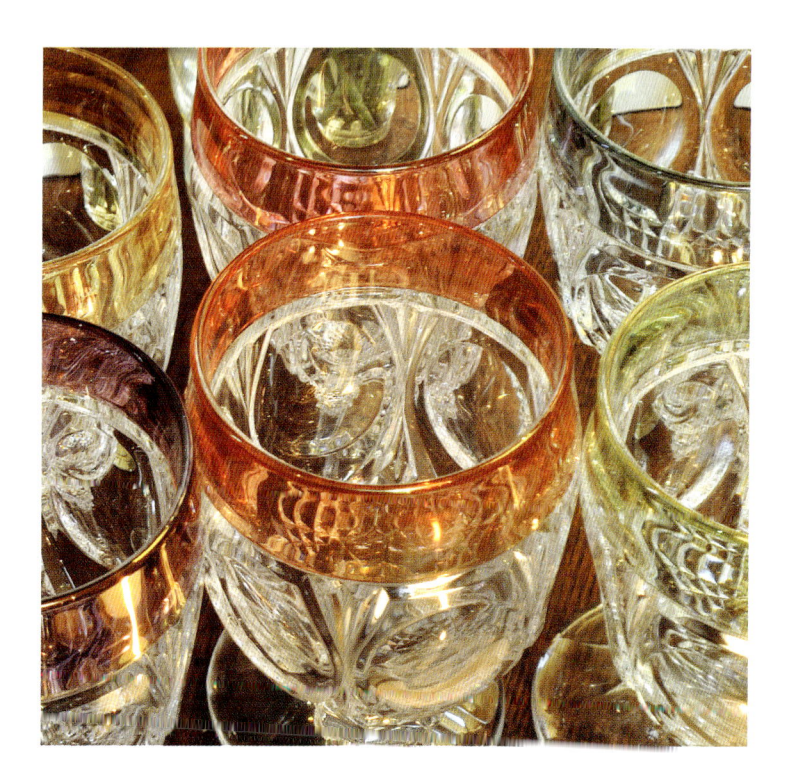

Whiskey Chocolate Cake

Excellent with coffee. A great way to end a party.

Serves 8

¼ cup raisins
½ cup whiskey
220g dark chocolate
3 tbsp water
½ cup butter
3 egg yolks
⅔ cup sugar
70g plain flour
⅔ cup ground almonds
3 egg whites

Method

1. Marinate raisins in whiskey for 2-3 hours.
2. Melt chocolate with water in a double-boiler and stir in butter in small pieces.
3. Beat egg yolks with sugar until pale and creamy.
4. Mix with chocolate and stir in flour and almonds.
5. Stir in raisins and whiskey.
6. Whip egg whites until they hold a soft peak.
7. With the mix, stir in a third, then fold in the rest.
8. Butter a round 23cm cake tin, line with greaseproof paper, butter and dust with flour.
9. Pour in cake mixture and bake at 190°C for 20 minutes.
10. This cake is best if it can sit overnight. Sprinkle with icing sugar.

White Chocolate Pannacotta with Raspberries

A delicious, easy dessert. You don't need to put it into moulds – you could just as easily leave the mixture loose and place lovely great dollops of it on top of berries of your choice.

Serves 6-8
200ml crème fraiche
250ml double cream
180g white chocolate
210g fresh raspberries

Method

1. Heat the crème fraiche with 100ml of the cream. Break the chocolate into a bowl and pour the hot cream over it. Leave for 1 minute, then stir to dissolve. Cover with cling film, spike a few air holes into it, and refrigerate for 2 hours.
2. Scatter the raspberries over the bottom of 6-8 ramekins.
3. Whisk the remaining cream until thick but soft and fold into the white chocolate mixture. Spoon over the raspberries, tap the ramekins to remove any air pockets and refrigerate for a few hours.
4. To serve: run a knife around the inside of the ramekins, dip bottoms briefly in hot water and turn out.

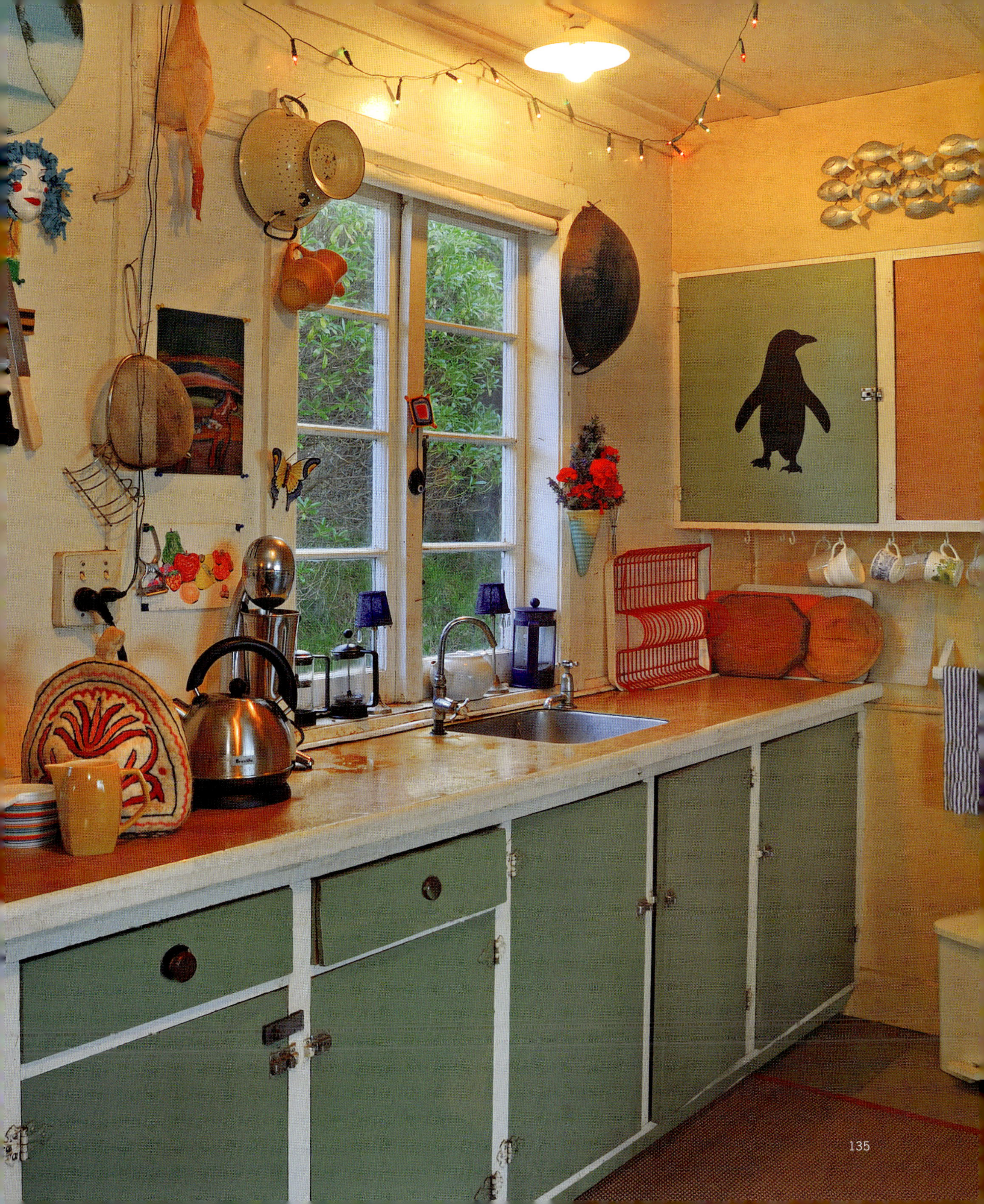

Glazed Lemon and Mascarpone Tart

What a tart! Rich and creamy, it is everything you need in a dessert. The filling is like crème brûlée but baked in a tart. Take the time to make your own sweet pastry.

Serves 8-10

Sweet pastry (see *Essentials*)
6 eggs
4 egg yolks
350g castor sugar
90g unsalted butter, softened
150g mascarpone, softened
Zest of 5 lemons
Juice of 6 lemons
Demerara sugar

Method

1. Line a 25cm tart tin with pastry, prick with a fork all over and chill for at least 20 minutes. Preheat oven to 200°C. Line with baking paper, fill with rice or beans and bake blind for 15 minutes on a tray.
2. Reduce oven to 180°C.
3. Whisk together eggs, egg yolks and sugar until light and fluffy. Make sure the sugar is dissolved.
4. Add butter, mascarpone, zest, and juice, mix well. Pour into the tart shell and bake for 30-40 minutes or until firm. Cool down then refrigerate.
5. Sprinkle sugar over the surface of the tart and place under a hot grill to caramelise.

Take the time to practise making your own pastry. It's invariably superior to bought pastry, and it is a truly satisfying moment when you master the art. Find a recipe that works for you and stick to it, you will only have to omit the sugar for a savoury pastry, adding perhaps a little herb or cheese.

"Downtown" Chocolate Mousse

My friends Dave and Gary gave me this recipe. It is everything a chocolate mousse should be…

>200g dark chocolate (Nestlé Club is good)
>2 eggs, separated
>50g unsalted butter, softened
>50g icing sugar
>300ml cream
>1 tbsp liqueur (optional) – Grand Marnier, Kahlua, etc.

Method
1. Break chocolate into small pieces and melt in a bowl over hot water (or in the microwave) with the butter.
2. Remove when combined and add egg yolks and liqueur.
3. Whip the cream with half the icing sugar until stiff.
4. Whip egg whites with remaining icing sugar.
5. Fold both into chocolate mixture.
6. Set the mixture in the fridge either in individual serving glasses or in a bowl and serve as ice-cream scoops.

Chocolate Almond Fudge Cake

The special thing about this cake apart from being absolutely divine, is that it will feed many people. I have often done it for parties with great success and, what's more, you can make it a few days in advance. It gets deeper and richer with time. Serve simply with a dollop of cream, and perhaps a little raspberry coulis. This gives the denseness an edge so that you end up with the perfect balance of flavours

Serves 10

250g butter
250g cooking chocolate
8 eggs, separated
250g castor sugar
250g ground almonds
150g cooking chocolate, to garnish

Method

1. Melt butter with chocolate. Cool.
2. Beat egg yolks with castor sugar until pale and thick.
3. Add the ground almonds, then stir in the cooled butter and chocolate.
4. Beat the egg whites until stiff. Fold them into the chocolate mixture.
5. Grease a 23cm or 25cm cake tin and pour in mixture.
6. Bake at 180°C for 50-55 minutes.
7. Allow to cool in the tin before turning out.
8. When cool, completely cover the top of the cake with melted chocolate.

Be careful when you are melting chocolate: if it becomes too hot, it will go grainy and there is absolutely nothing you can do except tip it down the sink (and even that could prove difficult).

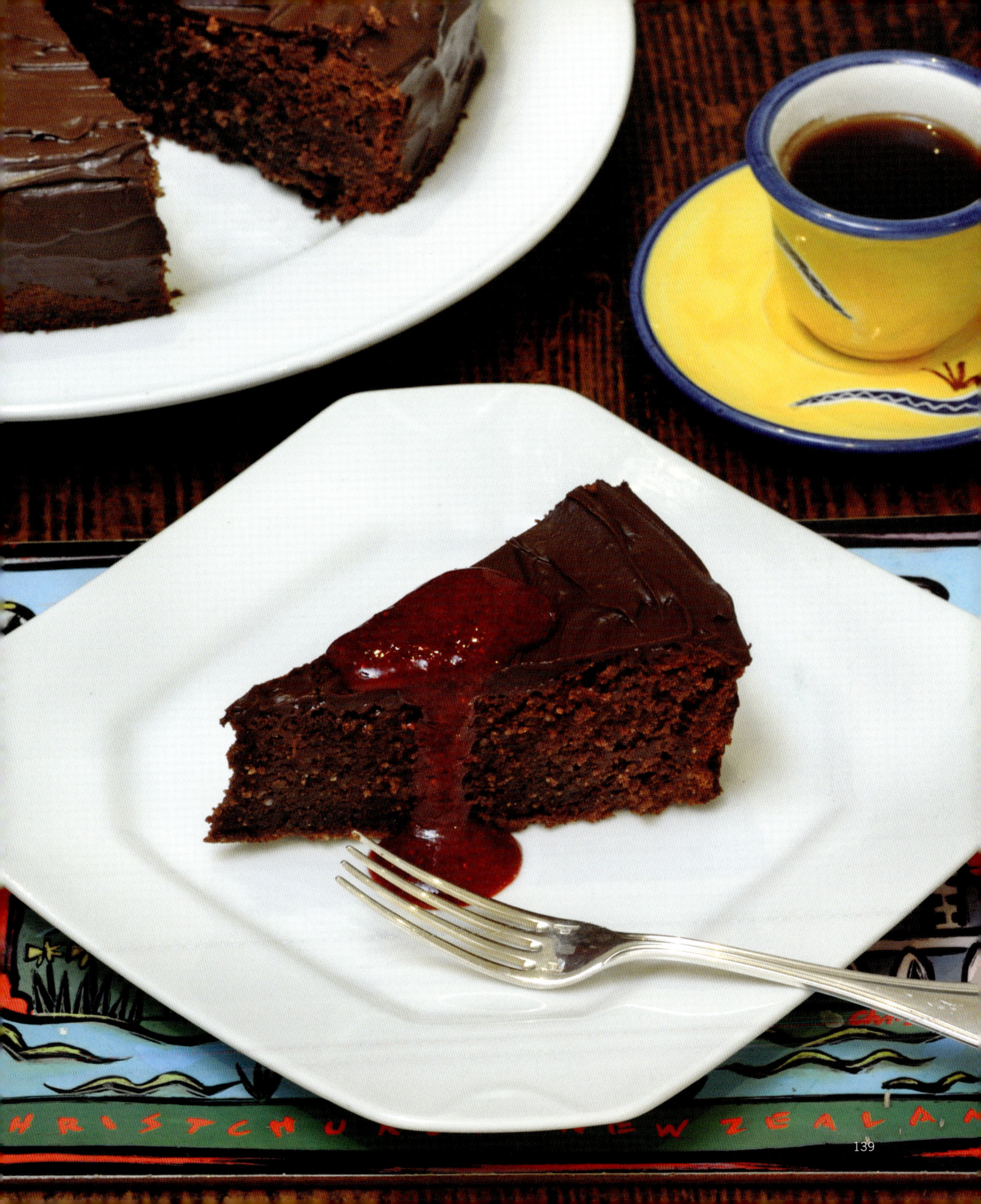

Lumberjack Cake

My friend Clare gave me this recipe. It's my husband's favourite cake. Of course you can make it with dried dates too.

Serves 6-8

1 cup chopped fresh dates
2 medium apples, peeled and grated
1 tsp baking soda
115g butter
1 cup castor sugar
1 egg
1 tsp vanilla essence
1½ cups flour
½ tsp salt

Topping:

50g butter
½ cup brown sugar
½ cup milk   } Mix together
½ cup coconut

Method

1. Turn oven to 180°C. Prepare a 20cm tin, buttered, floured and lined with paper.
2. Put dates, apples and soda into a bowl and cover with half a cup boiling water. Leave for 1 hour.
3. Cream butter and sugar, then add beaten egg and vanilla.
4. Stir in sifted flour and salt, then date and apple mixture. Combine and pour into prepared tin. Bake for 40 minutes.
5. Remove and spread on topping mixture. Return to oven for another 20 minutes.

'Cream butter and sugar': this step really is important. Those of us who do a lot of baking will confirm that the better and more thoroughly one combines these two ingredients, the better the end result will be.

Soft Te Mata Goat's Cheese and Berry Clafoutis

My friends Robert and Charlotte Fisher make this delicious cheese called Summerlea. I adore it – not only for its taste but for its versatility. Savoury or sweet by the addition of herbs or icing sugar, it is a top cheese. Here I have baked it with raspberries, but of course any fruit in season would be delicious.

Serves 6
500g fresh raspberries
250g soft goat's cheese
140g castor sugar
4 eggs
180g (1 ½ cups) almond meal

Method

1. Preheat the oven to 170°C. Grease one large 30cm or six half cup gratin dishes.
2. Place the raspberries in a single layer in the base of each gratin dish.
3. Place the goat's cheese, castor sugar, eggs and almond meal in a food processor and process to form a smooth mixture.
4. Pour the goat's cheese mixture over the berries. Bake for 20-25 minutes until the batter is raised and golden. Allow to cool down a little.
5. Dust the clafoutis with icing sugar and serve warm with lightly whipped cream.

BLACK DOG COTTAGE COOKBOOK

Essentials

Often a meal can be lifted out of the ordinary just by the addition of a salsa, dressing, pickle or a sauce. The recipes in this section are vital to the way I cook. It is for this reason that I always stock two or three pottles of different essential accompaniments in my fridge at once... not to mention a jar of aioli, which I am never without.

Create your own sauces with any vegetable that can be cooked, roasted and puréed or simply make a delicious mix of fresh raw greens of parsley, garlic, coriander and a little lemon to go with whatever it is you are serving. It is important to remember that these finishing touches do not "fight" with your meal but rather create a liaison, a bringing together of flavours. When you have some of these back-ups in your fridge or your pantry you can immediately give your food another layer of interest, another edge, subtle or profound.

I may travel with a jar of miso or lemon pickle, just in case I'm ever asked to cook ... if not, they make a beautiful and thoughtful gift.

Creole Spice

I have always got a jar of this spice sitting in my pantry, and especially now as I have a son who loves spicy food. Add it to the base of your sauce for pasta or put it over a fillet of fish or a piece of chicken before searing and cooking.

Makes about 2 cups

2 tsp dried oregano
¼ cup granulated garlic
¼ cup black pepper
1 tbsp cayenne pepper
2 tbsp white pepper
2 tbsp dried thyme
2 tbsp dried basil
75g paprika
3 tbsp granulated onion

Method

Combine all the above ingredients together and store in an airtight jar.

Miso Dressing

Delicious with avocado, tomatoes, chicken, and fish. If you want to make this thinner, simply add a little oil or water. This will fast become a necessity to have in your fridge.

- 1 shallot, chopped
- 2 garlic cloves, chopped
- 2 cm piece ginger, chopped
- 1 small chilli, seeds removed, and chopped
- ⅓ cup light oil
- ⅓ cup rice wine vinegar
- ¼ cup tahini
- ¼ cup brown miso
- 1 tsp kelp pepper
- 1 tbsp honey
- 3 tsp toasted sesame seeds

Method

1. Place first 4 ingredients in your food processor and chop on high for a bit. Then add the rest of the ingredients, apart from the sesame seeds. Proceed to blend until you have a lovely smooth dressing
2. Fold in sesame seeds and refrigerate.

Green Curry Paste

Still far superior to the bought paste. Always a gorgeous gift for someone into cooking and taste.

Makes about 1 cup

4 tbsp roughly chopped lemongrass

1 tbsp galangal, pre-soaked for 30 minutes

2 tbsp chopped garlic

1 medium sized onion, chopped

2 whole coriander plants, including roots and stems, chopped

1 tsp chopped lime or lemon zest

15 fresh green chillies

10 black peppercorns, cracked

2 tsp ground cumin

2 tsp shrimp paste

2 tsp ground coriander

1 tsp salt

3 cloves

3 bay leaves

2 tbsp vegetable oil for blending

Method

Blend or process all the ingredients together, using extra oil if necessary to achieve a smooth paste.

Lemon Pickle

A recipe from Pete Johnstone that I have adapted slightly. I use this lemon pickle on just about everything, from lamb to fish to a couscous salad.

Makes approximately 7 x 150ml jars

2 whole lemons, chopped and pips removed
5 large onions, roughly chopped
5-6 cloves garlic, crushed
4 cups white wine vinegar
1 cup lemon juice
3 tsp salt
5 cups sugar
1 tsp turmeric
4 tsp horseradish (peeled and grated, or bottled)
Finely grated rind of 2 lemons
2 tsp ground ginger
½ pkt jam-setting mix

Method

1. Roughly chop lemons, onions and garlic. Leave chunky.
2. Place in pot with all other ingredients (excluding the jam-setting mix) and bring to the boil.
3. Reduce heat and simmer for about 40 minutes.
4. Add jam-setting mix if you like a thicker pickle. Cook for another 5 minutes.
5. Bottle while hot in sterilised jars.

Horseradish Vinaigrette

A top vinaigrette. You'll use it and use it. Handy over anything and keeps well in the refrigerator.

30ml cider vinegar
1 heaped tsp Dijon mustard
1 tbsp grated horseradish or a good bottled one
½ tsp sugar
¾ tsp salt
¼ tsp white pepper
¾ cup grapeseed oil

Method
Blend all the ingredients together for the vinaigrette. Add some hot water to make a good pouring consistency.

Cashew Nut Mayo

I love cashew nut mayo, it's great with crudités, chicken and fish.

2 tbsp raw cashews
2 cloves garlic, crushed
1½ tsp seed mustard
2 tbsp soy sauce
2 tbsp lemon juice
½ cup water
1 tbsp extra virgin olive oil

Method
Place all ingredients in a blender and process until smooth.

Lime and Chilli Syrup

A fabulously easy little sauce to have in your fridge that only takes a jiffy to make. Excellent with prawns, scallops, noodles, pork or rice.

200g light palm sugar, finely grated
1 lime juiced, rind finely grated
1 large fresh red chilli, seeds removed, finely chopped
1 large fresh green chilli, seeds removed, finely chopped

Method

To make the syrup, heat the sugar and 150ml water in a saucepan over low-medium heat for 5 minutes, or just until the sugar and water start to caramelize. Remove from heat, add the lime juice and stir well. Set aside to cool, then add the grated lime rind and chillies.

Greek Dressing

3 tbsp extra virgin olive oil
1 tbsp red wine vinegar
1 tsp dried oregano
3 capers, finely chopped
1 tbsp flat-leaf parsley, chopped
Salt and freshly ground black pepper

Method

Place all the ingredients in a jar and shake.

Caper Sauce

Good sauce to use with fish or chicken.

Makes about 400 mls

100g day-old bread
100g capers, rinsed and drained
1 bunch flat-leaf parsley, finely chopped
1 bunch spring onions, finely chopped
2 garlic cloves, finely chopped
150ml extra virgin olive oil
100ml thick Greek yoghurt
1 egg yolk
Salt and pepper to taste

Method

1. Soak the stale bread in water, then squeeze out all the water.
2. Put the soaked bread into a blender or food processor with the capers. Purée.
3. While the motor is running, add the parsley, spring onions, and garlic. Pour in the olive oil bit by bit, then the yoghurt. Add the egg yolk and adjust the seasoning.

Asian Salsa

Great with beef or chicken, mixed with pasta, or served alongside oysters or seafood.

Serves 6

500g ripe tomatoes
1 cup spring onions, chopped
⅓ cup fresh basil, chopped
⅓ cup fresh mint
⅓ cup fresh coriander
3 cloves garlic, minced
3 tbsp lime juice
2 tbsp oil (light)
2 tbsp fish sauce
1½ tbsp light brown sugar
1½ tsp chilli sauce

Method

1. Cut tomatoes in half and remove seeds.
2. Chop onions, basil, mint, and coriander in food processor. Add tomatoes and chop again.
3. Combine with the remaining ingredients.

Pea Sauce

Made in a flash, keeps well, tastes yummy and works with most dishes.

Makes about 2 cups
Splash of olive oil
100g shallots, chopped
4 spring onions, chopped
Few sprigs of mint, shredded
200g frozen peas
300ml chicken stock
Maldon salt and white pepper

Method
1. Heat olive oil, add shallots and spring onions, and cook until soft.
2. Add mint, peas and chicken stock. Season with salt and pepper. Bring to the boil and simmer for a few minutes. Remove from the heat.
3. Drain when it has cooled slightly, keeping the cooking juices.
4. Place peas, mint, shallots and spring onions in the blender. Slowly add the cooking stock until you have the consistency of pouring cream. If you want a finer sauce, place through a sieve.

Warm Tomato Vinaigrette

Very simple, and yet very good. Fabulous with fish, chicken, spinach salad and pasta.

Makes about 400ml
6 medium tomatoes, seeded and diced
50ml red wine vinegar
120ml extra virgin olive oil
30g shallots, finely chopped
1 tbsp finely cut chives
Salt and pepper

Method
Mix all the ingredients together, and season to taste. Warm very gently.

Sweet & Sour Cucumber Relish

A beautiful complement to beef, ham, whitebait fritters, even asparagus.

Makes about 350mls
125ml vinegar
200g sugar
1 tsp salt
3 tbsp water
1 small onion, finely diced
1 small carrot, finely diced
1 medium cucumber, finely diced
Fresh coriander leaves, chopped

Method
1. Boil vinegar, sugar, salt and water for 1 minute.
2. Mix onion, carrot and cucumber in a bowl, pour over syrup so that vegetables are just covered. Add coriander.
3. Add a little chilli if you prefer a spicy relish and sprinkle with chopped coriander.

Tomato Concassé

Makes about 2 cups
Extra virgin olive oil
2 small onions, finely chopped
2 cloves garlic, crushed
1 tbsp dried tomato paste
2kg ripe tomatoes, seeded, skinned and roughly chopped

Method
1. Put a good glug of oil in a pan and soften the onion and garlic together. Add the tomato paste.
2. Let everything cook together for 5 minutes, then add your tomatoes. Reduce down until you have a beautiful thickish chunky tomato mixture left.

Lime Mayo

Makes about 3½ cups
5 tbsp fresh lime juice
2 egg yolks
2 tbsp Dijon mustard
3 cups vegetable oil
Grated zest of 2 limes
Freshly ground black pepper

Method
1. Place lime juice, eggs and mustard in food processor and process.
2. Add oil slowly until mayo has thickened.
3. Fold in lime zest and pepper.

Sweet Vinaigrette

I often take a jar of this away with me to the beach. Great over anything and everything, and for dipping bread into with a drink.

> 1 tbsp honey
> 1½ tbsp balsamic vinegar
> Maldon salt and freshly ground pepper
> 1 cup extra virgin olive oil

Method

1. Place honey and balsamic vinegar in a jar and put in the microwave. Heat for about 40 seconds.
2. Add seasoning and oil. Place lid on the jar and shake.

Nam Prik Num Sauce

Divine over noodles.

> 3 cloves garlic
> 1 chilli
> 2 cm piece ginger
> 2 handfuls of coriander
> 1 handful of parsley
> 1 can drained papaya
> Juice of a lime
> ¼ cup vinegar
> 1½ cups oil
> Salt and pepper

Method

1. Process garlic, chilli and ginger. Add coriander, parsley and process.
2. Then add papaya, lime juice, vinegar, oil and process again. Season.

Aioli

For me, no meal is complete without a dollop of aioli. I make mine with whole eggs as opposed to the classic French mayonnaise, which only uses the egg yolks. This version is somewhat lighter and the risk of it splitting is slim. There is no comparison between a home-made aioli to one purchased at a supermarket.

Makes about 2½ cups
2 whole eggs
1 heaped tsp mustard
Splash of white wine vinegar
Maldon salt and white pepper
4 cloves of garlic, smashed
2 cups of grapeseed oil
Juice of one lemon

Method
1. Chop the garlic first in your food processor.
2. Add eggs, mustard, vinegar, salt and pepper and process for about a minute. With the blades still running slowly, add the oil (you may require a little more oil, this depends on the size of the eggs). When it has reached your desired consistency add the juice of a lemon.

Aioli is one of my mainstayers that I have in my fridge all year-round. I tend to take it wherever I go. For me, it just kind of marries everything together. I can't do without it.

Sweet and Savoury Pastry

Using a food processor and with the pulsing action you can make a very successful pastry. Just don't overwork the dough or it will become tough. Once you begin to see it coming together, lift out the pastry and do the final "bringing together" with your own light touch. For the savoury version, simply omit the sugar.

This recipe is Sean Moran's, however, he does not use a food processor to make his pastry!

Makes enough for a 23cm x 3cm shell.

200g plain flour
1 large pinch salt
100g castor sugar
150g unsalted butter, coarsely grated
1 tbsp cold water

Method

1. Sift flour, salt and castor sugar into your food processor, place in grated butter and process using the pulsing action. When the mixture resembles breadcrumbs drizzle in the cold water.
2. Continue with the pulsing until you just see the mixture coming together. Lift out and continue to work, forming it into a flat disc. Wrap in cling film and refrigerate for about 1 hour.

Index

A
Aioli 156
    Roasted Fillet of Fish on Caramelised Onion and Fennel, Roasted Beetroot and Garlic with Warm Tomato Vinaigrette and Aioli 91
    Sweetcorn, Spring Onion and Coriander Risotto with Chicken Breast, Aioli and Lemon Pickle with an Asian Sauce 94
almonds
    Chocolate Almond Fudge Cake 138
    Summer Cake with Raspberry and Almond 124
Asian
    Asian Salsa 151
asparagus 23
aubergines
    Spaghetti with Aubergine, Chilli and Tomato 114

B
baba ghanoush
    Mezze Plate of Baba Ghanoush, Hummus, Tzatziki, Roasted Olives and Tomato Salad 15
beans
    Giant Baked Beans with Tomatoes and Dill 63
beef
    Beef Chilli with Salsa 113
    Marinated Japanese Beef with Spring Onions 22
    Roasted Sirloin Strip with Watercress, Cos and Beetroot Salad 105
berries
    Mascarpone and Raspberry Crème Brûlée 123
    Roasted Nectarines with Berries and Mascarpone 132
    Soft Te Mata Goat's Cheese and Berry Clafoutis 141
    Summer Cake with Raspberry and Almond 124
    White Chocolate Pannacotta with Raspberries 134
bouquet garnis 18
Briam 49
Broad Bean, Pea, Asparagus, Spring Onion and Herbs 72

C
cake
    Chocolate Almond Fudge Cake 138
    Lumberjack Cake 110
    Rules for Making Cakes 122
    Summer Cake with Raspberry and Almond 124
    Whiskey Chocolate Cake 133
Caponata 59
Celeriac Rémoulade 71
cheese
    Prawns with Tomatoes and Feta 102
    Soft Te Mata Goat's Cheese and Berry Clafoutis 141

chicken
    A bit of a Greek Chicken with Potatoes 87
    Chicken Stock 37
    Fab Chook Pie 116
    Fried Noodles with Chicken and Shrimps 83
    Pilaf of Spinach, Dill and Marinated Grilled Chicken Breast 96
    Sesame Chicken with Warm Noodles 112
    Tandoori Chicken 104
    Thai Chicken Noodle Soup 38
    Thai-High Chicken Livers 27
Chickpeas with Tomato and Chilli 25
chilli
    Beef Chilli with Salsa 113
    Chickpeas with Tomato and Chilli 25
    Spaghetti with Aubergine, Chilli and Tomato 114
chocolate
    Chocolate Almond Fudge Cake 138
    "Downtown" Chocolate Mousse 137
    Whiskey Chocolate Cake 133
    White Chocolate Pannacotta with Raspberries 134
clafoutis
    Peach Clafoutis 131
    Soft Te Mata Goat's Cheese and Berry Clafoutis 141
concassé
    Grilled Fish with Mustard and Anchovy Hollandaise and Tomato Concassé 85
    Tomato Concassé 154
crème brûlée
    Mascarpone and Raspberry Crème Brûlée 123
cucumber
    Sweet & Sour Cucumber Relish 153
curry
    Green Curry Paste 146
    Green Fish Curry 88
    Swordfish Curry 107

D
dates
    Sticky Date Pudding 127
Doris Slater School of Cooking 110
dressing
    Greek Dressing 149
    Grilled Vegetable and Pasta Salad with Lemon Mustard Dressing 52
    Miso Dressing 145
    Warm Salad of New Potatoes, Cauliflower, Broccoli and Asparagus with Mint and Parsley Honey Dressing 48
duck
    Duck Breast With Szechwan Rub 89
    Wild Duck Ragout 109

E
Essentials 143

F
Family & Friends 81
Fava 33
filo
　Filo-Wrapped Asparagus And Parma Ham 23
fish
　Baked Snapper with Vegetables 117
　Cooking Fish 98
　Grilled Fish with Mustard and Anchovy Hollandaise and Tomato Concassé 85
　Philly's Fish Pie 82
　Seared Swordfish, Lemon Salsa Verde, Garlic, Potato and Rocket Mash 99
　Seared Tuna in Soy and Mirin 32
　Sumac-spiced Tuna Salad 75
　Swordfish Curry 107
fritters
　Asian Prawn Fritters 26
　Thai Whitebait Fritters 29
　Zucchini Fritters – Greek Style 18

H
hummus
　Mezze Plate of Baba Ghanoush, Hummus, Tzatziki, Roasted Olives and Tomato Salad 15

I
ice cream
　Semifreddo Nougat Ice Cream 128

J
Jambalaya 84

L
lamb
　Aegean Lamb 92
　Lamb and Vegetable Barley Broth 44
　Lamb Harira 39
　Preserved Lemon Marinated Leg of Lamb 118
lentils
　Puy Lentils with Sautéed Vegetables 50
Light Dishes 17
liver
　Thai-High Chicken Livers 27

M
marinade
　Pilaf of Spinach, Dill and Marinated Grilled Chicken Breast 96

mascarpone
　Glazed Lemon and Mascarpone Tart 136
　Mascarpone and Raspberry Crème Brûlée 123
　Roasted Nectarines with Berries and Mascarpone 132
mayo
　Cashew Nut Mayo 148
　Lime Mayo 154
Mezze 11
　Mezze Plate of Baba Ghanoush, Hummus, Tzatziki, Roasted Olives and Tomato Salad 15
mirin
　Seared Tuna in Soy and Mirin 32
Miso Dressing 145
mousse
　"Downtown" Chocolate Mousse 137

N
nectarines
　Roasted Nectarines with Berries and Mascarpone 132
noodles
　Fried Noodles with Chicken and Shrimps 83
　Sesame Chicken with Warm Noodles 112
　Thai Noodle Salad 58

O
octopus
　My Greek Octopus 13

P
Paella 108
pannacotta
　White Chocolate Pannacotta with Raspberries 134
parma ham
　Filo-Wrapped Asparagus And Parma Ham 23
pasta
　Grilled Vegetable and Pasta Salad with Lemon Mustard Dressing 52
pastry
　Rosti with Pastry Topping 76
　Sweet and Savoury Pastry 157
pickle
　Lemon Pickle 147
pies
　Fab Chook Pie 116
　Philly's Fish Pie 82
pineapple
　Grilled Pineapple 125
Pissaladiere 30
potatoes
　A bit of a Greek Chicken with Potatoes 87
prawns
　Asian Prawn Fritters 26
　Prawns with Tomatoes and Feta 102
pudding
　Sticky Date Pudding 127
　Summer Pudding 126

R

ragout
    Wild Duck Ragout   109
rémoulade
    Celeriac Rémoulade   71
Rosti with Pastry Topping   76

S

salad
    Cannellini Bean, Corn and Fresh Herb Salad   60
    'Greeky' Aubergine, Coriander and Roasted Walnut Salad   68
    Grilled Vegetable and Pasta Salad with Lemon Mustard Dressing   52
    Hydra Salad   74
    Mezze Plate of Baba Ghanoush, Hummus, Tzatziki, Roasted Olives and Tomato Salad   15
    Niçoise Salad Sauce   64
    Roasted Sirloin Strip with Watercress, Cos and Beetroot Salad   105
    Shitake and Celery Heart Salad with Muscatels and Walnuts   55
    Sumac-spiced Tuna Salad   75
    Thai Carrot Salad   53
    Thai Noodle Salad   58
    Warm Salad of New Potatoes, Cauliflower, Broccoli and Asparagus with Mint and Parsley Honey Dressing   48
    Warm Sweet Corn Salad   57
salsa
    Beef Chilli with Salsa   113
    Seared Swordfish, Lemon Salsa Verde, Garlic, Potato and Rocket Mash   99
sauce
    Asian Sauce   94
    Caper Sauce   150
    Nam Prik Num Sauce   155
    Niçoise Salad Sauce   64
    Pea Sauce   152
semifreddo
    Semifreddo Nougat Ice Cream   128
shrimps
    Fried Noodles with Chicken and Shrimps   83
soups   35
    Chickpea, Leek And Roasted Tomato Soup   41
    Green Minestrone   45
    Lamb and Vegetable Barley Broth   44
    Mushroom Soup   40
    Thai Chicken Noodle Soup   30
Souvlaki   17
soy
    Seared Tuna in Soy and Mirin   32
spaghetti
    Spaghetti with Aubergine, Chilli and Tomato   114
spice
    Creole Spice   144
spinach
    Pilaf of Spinach, Dill and Marinated Grilled Chicken Breast   96

spring onions
    Marinated Japanese Beef with Spring Onions   22
stocks
    Chicken Stock   37
Sweet Things   121
syrup
    Lime and Chilli Syrup   149

T

tart
    Glazed Lemon and Mascarpone Tart   136
terrine
    Mediterranean Vegetable Terrine   79
thai
    Thai Carrot Salad   53
    Thai Chicken Noodle Soup   38
    Thai-High Chicken Livers   27
    Thai Noodle Salad   58
    Thai Whitebait Fritters   29
tomatoes
    Chickpea, Leek And Roasted Tomato Soup   41
    Chickpeas with Tomato and Chilli   25
    Giant Baked Beans with Tomatoes and Dill   63
    Grilled Fish with Mustard and Anchovy Hollandaise and Tomato Concassé   85
    Mezze Plate of Baba Ghanoush, Hummus, Tzatziki, Roasted Olives and Tomato Salad   15
    Prawns with Tomatoes and Feta   102
    Spaghetti with Aubergine, Chilli and Tomato   114
    Tomato Concassé   154
    Warm Tomato Vinaigrette   152
tortilla
    Rocket and Feta Tortilla   54
tuna
    Seared Tuna in Soy and Mirin   32
tzatziki
    Mezze Plate of Baba Ghanoush, Hummus, Tzatziki, Roasted Olives and Tomato Salad   15

V

vinaigrette
    Horseradish Vinaigrette   148
    Roasted Fillet of Fish on Caramelised Onion And Fennel, Roasted Beetroot and Garlic with Warm Tomato Vinaigrette and Aioli   91
    Sweet Vinaigrette   155
    Warm Tomato Vinaigrette   152

W

whitebait
    Thai Whitebait Fritters   29

Z

Zucchini Fritters – Greek Style   18